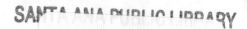

CULTURES OF THE WORLD

SWITZERLAND

Zum Schlüssel

Patricia Levy

MARSHALL CAVENDISH
New York • London • Sydney

Reference edition published 1994 by
Marshall Cavendish Corporation
2415 Jerusalem Avenue
P.O. Box 587
North Bellmore
New York 11710

© Times Editions Pte Ltd 1994

Originated and designed by
Times Books International, an imprint of
Times Editions Pte Ltd

Printed in Malaysia

Library of Congress Cataloging-in-Publication Data:
Levy, Patricia Marjorie.
    Switzerland / Patricia Levy.
      p. cm.—(Cultures Of The World)
    Includes bibliographical references and index.
    ISBN 1-85435-591-0
    1. Switzerland—Juvenile literature [1. Switzerland.]
I. Title. II. Series.
DQ17.L47 1994
914.9404'73—dc20   93–44260
              CIP
              AC

Cultures of the World

Editorial Director	Shirley Hew
Managing Editor	Shova Loh
Editors	Tan Kok Eng
	Roseline Lum
	Michael Spilling
	Winnifred Wong
	Guek-Cheng Pang
	Sue Sismondo
Picture Editor	Mee-Yee Lee
Production	Edmund Lam
Design	Tuck Loong
	Ronn Yeo
	Felicia Wong
	Loo Chuan Ming
Illustrators	Eric Chew
	Lok Kerk Hwang
	William Sim
	Wong Nok Sze
MCC Editorial Director	Evelyn M. Fazio

INTRODUCTION

SET AMID STUNNING MOUNTAIN RANGES and flanked on all sides by its neighbors, Switzerland is a country of enormous contrasts. From bustling urban centers and dynamic financial hubs, the visitor can travel in a couple of hours to tiny Alpine hamlets where villagers' lives revolve around raising cows. Switzerland values its neutrality, yet has the most easily mobilized, highly armed, citizen soldiery in the world. Its industries range from high technology to textiles and tourism; its weather from areas of year-long snow to Mediterranean heat. In 700 years as a nation, Switzerland has produced important artists, writers, and thinkers, and has provided a safe haven for people forced to flee their own countries in times of war.

This book, part of the *Cultures of the World* series, provides insights into the lives of the Swiss, how they work and play, their beliefs, culture, and aspirations. It offers a more detailed picture of Switzerland than what the average tourist may see.

CONTENTS

A medieval warrior stands guard in front of a building in Stein am Rhein, northeast Switzerland.

CONTENTS

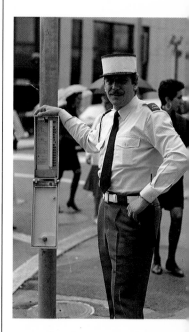

A Swiss police officer
sees that public order is
kept.

GEOGRAPHY

LIKE ITS IMMEDIATE NEIGHBOR, AUSTRIA, Switzerland is a landlocked country. It is bordered on the west by France, on the north by Germany, on the east by Austria and the tiny principality of Liechtenstein, and on the south by Italy.

It is one of the smallest countries in Europe, both in terms of area and population. Covering 15,943 square miles, it has a population of only 6,674,000, including one million immigrants, but its position at the center of Europe makes it a very significant country.

To the northwest of Switzerland is the region known as the Jura, a rolling mountain range, while to the southeast are the Swiss Alps. Between the two mountain ranges lies the Mittelland, the hub of the country where the bulk of the population lives.

Opposite: **Resort dwellings nestle in the Alpine valley of Arosa, in eastern Switzerland. The entire area here is mountainous, containing peaks and glaciers. A tourist industry thrives around the many spas and resorts.**

Below: **Besides drawing millions of skiers to the area every year, the snow-covered Alps provide Switzerland with a vital resource—water. Switzerland has over a thousand lakes and many rivers.**

With a length of 14.6 miles, the Aletsch is the largest glacier in the Alps. The glaciers of the Alps are monitored systematically because their growth or decline are evidence of subtle climatic changes.

THE ALPS

The Alps are a crescent-shaped range of mountains beginning in southeast France and extending across southern Switzerland into Austria. They are the largest mountain range in Europe. Three-fifths of Switzerland's landmass is covered by the Alps, but fewer than one-fifth of its people live there.

The Alps were formed in two stages, millions of years ago. First, a period of mountain building about 30 million years ago thrust up great arches of rock that buckled over, creating the distinctive rock formations still visible today. Then, a second episode of mountain building thrust the whole chain even higher. Millions of years of erosion, followed by excavation by the great glaciers of the last Ice Age, created the tortuous shapes of today's Alps. The peaks of the Alps stood above the glaciers and were unaffected by them, but the glaciers filled the whole Mittelland region. Other glaciers carved out the valleys of the Alps. Where the glaciers

AVALANCHES

Avalanches are caused when snow is dislodged from the mountainside by a tremor or disturbance. They are most likely to occur when the gradient or slope of the mountainside is more than 22 degrees. An avalanche can reach speeds of up to 200 m.p.h. The air pushed along in front of the avalanche can cause as much damage as the avalanche itself. The Alpine region of Switzerland has about 10,000 avalanches a year, mostly during February, March, and April. The pine forests high up on the mountains can hold back the snow slides, but for additional safety, many artificial structures have been built along the most susceptible stretches of roads and around Alpine villages. With the enormous increase in winter sports over recent years and the large numbers of tourists who could be affected by snowfalls, a special avalanche report is now prepared daily during the winter months.

finally disappeared, they left behind great mounds of debris that blocked the rivers and created the beautiful lakes of Switzerland.

Today, the Alps contain over 1,000 glaciers that are still at work carving out ever deeper valleys. Compared to the great glaciers of the last Ice Age, however, these are tiny. The largest of them is the Aletsch Glacier, near Bern, which is 14.6 miles long.

The Alps are the source of many of Europe's major rivers. The high mountains with sharp inclines and the bountiful supply of water give Switzerland one of its greatest natural assets—hydroelectric power. The upper valleys of two rivers, the Rhine and the Rhone, divide the Alps into a northern and southern range of mountains.

The appearance of the mountains varies according to the height and degree of exposure to winds. As high as 4,923 feet, the land is used for agriculture; above this are coniferous forests. Above the tree line, at about 7,200 feet, the mountain pastures begin. Beyond 9,842 feet little can grow, except a few mosses and lichens that cling to the bare rocks.

The highest point in Switzerland is the Dufourspitze at 15,203 feet. The Matterhorn, with its distinctive outline, is slightly lower at 14,691 feet.

The hamlet of La Bosse lies 3,300 feet above sea level on the high-lying plateau of the Jura Fribourg. Pastures are more characteristic on the high plateaus of the Jura than the cultivated fields more commonly seen in the basins and valleys.

THE JURA

The Jura ("YOOR-ah") covers 160 miles of the French-Swiss border. The highest point of this mountain range is Crêt de la Neige, in France, at 5,652 feet.

Jura is a Celtic word meaning "forest." The mountain range was formed by the same massive earth movements that built the Alps. It is thought that this earth movement, whose effects were felt all over Europe and beyond, was caused when the continents of Europe and Africa collided. The Jura Mountains are lower than the Alps. While the Alps are made up of a large variety of materials, the Jura Mountains are quite consistent; they are made up of sandstone, limestone, and marl. They also contain many fossils, which tells us that a long time ago these mountains lay beneath a shallow sea. In fact, this mountain range gives its name to a period of geological time—the Jurassic. The fossils found in the Jura Mountains are believed to be imprints of creatures from the Jurassic period.

While the peaks of the Alps escaped the rounding and weathering effects of the Ice Age, the Jura Mountains, being much lower, did not; thus they are characteristically rounded in shape. The tops of the mountains are sparsely forested because they are above the tree line, but the valleys are wooded. Plateaus created by the erosion of the mountains provide good farming land. One such plateau, the Franches-Montagnes, lies just east of Switzerland's border with France.

While the Alps are cut through by the many river systems that give travelers easy access across the mountains, the Jura Mountains have few natural interruptions. This makes travel across them difficult and the area has historically been a barrier to settlement.

The Mittelland is the backbone of the Swiss economy. Two-thirds of the country's population lives in this region.

THE MITTELLAND

Deposits accumulated from the erosion of the Alps over millions of years gradually formed the Mittelland region of Switzerland. The Mittelland, too, was carved by glaciers, but much more gently, to form rolling hills and valleys. Lake Geneva and Lake Constance were formed here as the glaciers hollowed out the lake beds and then melted, leaving the glacial deposits called moraines to block the paths of the meltwater. The Mittelland's average altitude is about 1,500 feet above sea level.

The Mittelland makes up about 30% of Switzerland's landmass. It supports the greater part of Switzerland's population and is the base for Switzerland's economic success. Most Swiss cities are in this region.

The Rhine flows through the Swiss city of Basel and on to the North Sea.

RIVER SYSTEMS AND LAKES

Switzerland is considered the hydrographic center of Europe. Both the Rhine and the Rhone, two of Europe's biggest rivers, have their sources here. The meltwater from the Alps and the Jura Mountains provides the starting point for these great rivers that so many countries in Europe depend on.

The Rhine rises in the Alps and flows first into Lake Constance. As it moves toward the lake, it carries meltwater and mountain streams with it; when it arrives at Lake Constance it is heavily burdened with debris, mud, and gravel. This material remains in the lake: the Rhine emerges again from Lake Constance a green and steady-moving river. The Rhine forms a natural boundary between Switzerland and Germany as far west as Basel, where it leaves Switzerland and begins its journey across Germany.

The Rhone rises in the Rhone glacier in the Furkapass in the Alps, only a few miles from the source of the Rhine. It descends westward toward Lake Geneva, where it deposits all the material it has carried from the mountainside. At Lake Geneva, it leaves Switzerland behind and becomes a French river, traveling the rest of its journey south along the Jura Mountains until it meets the Saône River.

Two other important rivers that have their sources in Switzerland are the Ticino River, which flows south from the Alps, and the Reuss River, which flows northward.

The enormous potential power of Switzerland's glaciers and river systems has been effectively harnessed in hydroelectric power stations that use underground tunnels to carry water and generate electricity. Two of the highest dams in Europe are in Switzerland. They are the Mauvoisin Dam at 777 feet and the Grande Dixence Dam at 932 feet. Both are on the higher reaches of the Rhone River and are very efficient sources of electrical power.

Lake Geneva is formed by the Rhone River. Prehistoric dwellings have been found on the shores of the lake.

The Swiss lakes are a major tourist attraction. Lake Geneva, also known as Lac Leman, is a crescent-shaped lake in the west of Switzerland that forms part of the border between Switzerland and France. It is the largest of Switzerland's lakes and is nine miles at its widest point. Several of Switzerland's larger cities are sited around the lake, including of course Geneva itself. A fleet of ships is maintained on the lake.

Lake Constance forms the eastern boundary of the Mittelland and Switzerland and part of the border with Germany and Austria. The second largest lake in Switzerland, it is about 40 miles long and 10 miles wide. Its position between the borders gives it a long history as a center for smuggling, but nowadays it is more important as a tourist center. It is unlike Switzerland's many other lakes in that it is not surrounded by mountains. The town of Constance lies partly in Germany and partly in Switzerland, and border points exist across the streets of the town.

MAJOR CITIES

ZURICH Although it is not the capital of Switzerland, Zurich is its largest city and the one that many people believe is the heart of Switzerland. Its dialect, *Schwyzerdütsch* ("SHVEET-zur-dootch"), or Swiss German, is the language used by the media. The economic, industrial, and cultural center of the country, it has a population of over 400,000. Its chief industries are banking and finance, commerce, engineering, electrical appliances, textiles, and tourism. Built around Lake Zurich and the river Limmat, Zurich has been a member of the Swiss Confederation since 1351.

BERN This is the federal capital of Switzerland, with a population of around 150,000. It too is a major industrial center, home to the pharmaceutical industry, the chocolate-making industry, and the graphic trades. It has been a member of the Swiss Confederation since 1353, two years less than Zurich. The older part of the city is perched high up on a ridge, in

Bern's history is pre-
served in fine old streets
and buildings. It is a historical center rather than
a modern cultural one,
and has many museums.

a loop of the Aare River. Much of this medieval city is preserved and is a heritage center. Characteristic of the city's shopping centers are arcades that stretch out over the sidewalk, offering pedestrians protection against harsh weather.

GENEVA Located at the far western border of Switzerland, Geneva is the home of many international organizations, including the Red Cross and some of the administrative sections of the United Nations. It was one of the last of the Swiss cantons (states*) to join the Swiss Confederation, being a free city until 1814. Built around Lake Geneva and the Rhone, its major industries include banking, precision instruments, and chemicals. It is the operational base of over 200 international organizations.

BASEL Situated on the borders of France, Germany, and Switzerland, and sited on the banks of the Rhine, Basel is an important center of communications, commerce, and chemical manufacturing. It is the second largest city in Switzerland, with 190,000 residents. Many of Switzerland's imported goods enter the country via Basel, being transported up the Rhine from Germany and beyond. A very prosperous city, Basel is home to many of Switzerland's millionaires. The Rhine River and its six bridges dominate the city, giving it an almost nautical air, as great barges ply up and down the river.

* See p. 34 for a detailed explanation of this term.

CLIMATE

Switzerland's climate varies from area to area because of the enormous differences in altitude and the effects of the mountains.

As the land rises, temperatures fall by 3°F for each 1,000 feet. Strangely, in the Mittelland and the Alpine valleys, the weather is damper and cloudier than above the cloud line in the high Alps, where the air is dry and there is frequent sunshine. The Swiss Alps have long been a choice location for sanatoriums, where people with various illnesses can recuperate in the dry, sunny winter air.

In the summer, the Mittelland is warm and sunny, with temperatures of around 65°F to 70°F. The sheltered valleys of the Jura and the Alps become uncomfortably hot during the summer months, while the upper slopes are cool. In the region of the Alps that extends toward Italy, the climate is more Mediterranean, with hot summers and mild winters.

Switzerland has high precipitation, which falls as rain or snow. The Mittelland gets around 45 inches of rain per year, while in the higher areas 100 inches of rain per year is common. Above 6,000 feet, snow covers the ground for at least six months of the year.

A large-horned mountain goat, the ibex can cling easily to rocky surfaces. It is an excellent climber and jumper that lives above the tree line most of the year.

FLORA AND FAUNA

One of Switzerland's greatest natural assets is its many thousands of forests. Fortunately for Switzerland, while other European countries cut down their native oaks and other trees for industry and firewood, the Swiss saw the value of planting.

There are both deciduous and pine forests. The deciduous forests grow largely in the Jura region, while the mountains of the Alps are covered in natural or planted forests of spruce, larch, and arolla pine trees. The larch is a very interesting tree, for unlike the other conifers, it sheds its leaves in winter. The typical woodland floor of the larch forest is grassy, with many wild flowers that bloom early in the season.

Many of the rarer plants of the Swiss Alps are protected by law. The edelweiss is a famous plant that grows high above the tree line in the mountains. It flowers from July to September. Like most other Alpine plants, it has large colorful flowers due to the high proportion of ultraviolet light in the upper slopes of the mountains. Other rare Alpine plants are the gentianella, the Alpine pansy, the aster, and the blue thistle.

Switzerland's wildlife is varied and beautiful. But with the encroachment of urban areas, greater use by tourists, and the Swiss love of hunting, many species have become endangered.

In 1914, the Swiss National Park was formed in the Engadine area of the Grisons and some degree of protection was given to the wild creatures of the area. Deer that were very rare in the early 20th century have now increased to the point where their presence endangers the survival of some plant species. The ibex, the national animal of the Grisons, were wiped out entirely in the last century but were reintroduced and are once again wandering the slopes outside the National Park. The chamois, a small goat-like antelope, also lives freely in the Alps. It was hunted in earlier times for its soft skin, which was used to make clothing.

Wild flowers bloom in the Alpine valleys of Switzerland. The valleys are home to many plants, including the dandelion and the cornflower.

17

CE FRAGMENT DE MOSAIQVE
A ETE PLACE EN CET ENDROIT
EN 1939
AVEC L'APPVI DES AVTORITES

HISTORY

EVIDENCE OF HUMANKIND'S EXISTENCE in Switzerland dates back 50,000 years. A fragment of a woman's jawbone, probably Neanderthal, was found in the Jura region. Pictorial evidence of human endeavor about 15,000 years ago has been found in the mountain caves of the Jura. Later, around 1500 B.C., communities of pre-Bronze Age people settled in the fertile plateau in villages of log huts built on the shores of lakes. Tools of bone and stone were found, showing that these communities had not yet discovered the use of metals.

By the time of the late Iron Age, a great new center of culture had emerged on the north bank of Lake Neuchâtel. This was the La Tène civilization of the Celts, a warlike race that swept across Europe, pushing back the more primitive Bronze Age cultures as they went. The Celts dominated Europe for centuries before being overtaken themselves by the might and power of the Roman Empire. In Switzerland, the Celts lived in the area between Lake Constance and Lake Geneva, on the Jura, and in the Alps.

Opposite: **Roman mosaic on a Swiss castle wall.**

Below: **Neuchâtel, the site of the Celtic La Tène civilization. The first Swiss coins came into existence during the La Tène civilization, around 800 B.C.**

A statue of Julius Caesar stands in the Roman Museum in Nyon, in the canton of Vaud. Roman rule in Switzerland lasted 400 years.

UNDER FOREIGN RULE

By the time recorded history began, the Celts in Switzerland, called Helvetians, were facing border threats by powerful tribes from Germany. In March 58 B.C., the Helvetians tried to emigrate to that part of Gaul that is now France. Unfortunately they found their way barred by the Romans under Julius Caesar, then governor of Gaul.

The Romans' concern was that if the Helvetians moved away, there would be no barrier between the Roman Empire and the waves of invading Germanic peoples. The Romans stopped the Helvetians at ancient Bibracte in Burgundy (southeast France) and defeated them. The Helvetians were forced to return to what was to be called Helvetia ("hehl-VAYT-see-ah"), the area between Lake Constance and Lake Geneva. They were promised protection from the Germanic peoples by the Romans, and Helvetia became a semi-independent part of the massive Roman Empire. Under the Romans, Helvetia developed rapidly. Road networks were built, towns were reestablished, and agriculture flourished.

A region to the east of Helvetia was inhabited by people called Etruscan Rhaetians. They spoke a language of their own and lived in what was to become the Grisons canton of Switzerland. They too formed a liaison with the Roman Empire, and the modern Romansh ("roh-MANCH") language of today is a mixture of their original language and Latin.

Switzerland was thus very important to the Romans. The borders of the Roman Empire lay north of Switzerland along the Rhine and Danube rivers, and the mountains of Switzerland formed the line along where they could fall back to if the Germanic tribes began to push forward. Cities developed, notably Aventicum (now Avenches). Palaces, temples, and triumphal arches have been excavated in that area inside the city walls.

But as the Roman Empire collapsed, the Germanic tribes moved into the northern parts of Switzerland and took possession, while the French Burgundians seized the south. Other southern parts of Switzerland came under the influence of Italy. By the fifth century, four different power groups developed, each with its own language: the Germanics in the north, the Burgundians and Lombards (Italians) in the south, and the Rhaetians in the east.

In the sixth century, Switzerland became part of another great empire, the Frankish kingdom ruled by Emperor Clovis. He had sworn to convert to Christianity if he could defeat the German tribes. He did, on Christmas Day A.D. 496. Christianity had already arrived in Switzerland a century earlier, but it had been put down by various rulers.

The Roman legacy can still be seen in many structures that are scattered across Switzerland. Road networks such as this viaduct were constructed to facilitate the movements of people and goods.

By A.D. 771, Switzerland was part of another empire, the Holy Roman Empire under the Emperor Charles, later called Charlemagne. It was under his rule that the modern cantons of Switzerland were largely created. Like the other empires before it, the Holy Roman Empire became too big to be efficiently managed, and by the time of Charlemagne's grandson in A.D. 834, Switzerland was again split into four separate units. It was not until 1032 that the Swiss territories were once more brought under a single ruler, the Holy Roman Emperor Conrad II. During the 12th century, Switzerland was again divided up and fought over. By 1291, Switzerland had come under the power of the House of Habsburg, which was to reign supreme throughout central Europe.

THE FOUNDATION OF MODERN SWITZERLAND

As an outcome of the increased power of the Habsburgs, a desire for autonomy and freedom was born in some of the cantons that would later become Switzerland. For the first time they saw a common goal of independence from emperors.

In 1291, Emperor Rudolf of Habsburg died, and in the vacuum created by his death, some of the Swiss cantons decided to act. Three of them, Uri, Schwyz, and Unterwalden drew up an agreement called the "Perpetual League," pledging mutual aid and allegiance among the three communities. Guerrilla attacks began on the bailiffs and soldiers of the Habsburg Empire. One of the Habsburg dukes led a force against the united cantons in 1315, but was defeated by them. This led to a whole spate of other cantons joining the Confederation—Lucerne in 1332, Zurich in 1351, Glarus and Zug in 1352, and Bern in 1353. More Habsburg attacks were defeated in 1386 and 1388, and in 1394 they signed a 20-year peace treaty.

THE EARLY CHRISTIANS

One of the first groups of Christians to arrive in Switzerland was a band of Irish monks, led by Columban, in A.D. 610. An early chronicle described the monks as long-haired and tattooed, carrying stout sticks, and a spare pair of boots around their necks. They traveled around Switzerland throwing carved images of gods into the rivers and causing havoc among the Swiss peoples, who resented their high-handed attempts to Christianize them. Driven out of the lakeside village of Tuggan, they moved into Brigantium (modern Bregenz) and began to smash heathen gods. Again ordered out of the area, the monks moved into Italy, leaving behind one of their number, Gall. Too sick to make the journey, Gall stayed in the forest of Arbon and in A.D. 614, founded the monastery of St. Gallen.

WILLIAM TELL

No one can quite decide whether William Tell is Swiss history or Swiss myth. Whichever it is, it is a good tale and one that is as much a part of the character of Switzerland as Swiss cheese or cuckoo clocks.

William Tell's story begins during the reign of the Emperor Rudolf. His canton was governed by the ruthless Habsburg supervisor Gessler, who, the story goes, put his hat on a pole in the town center and made everybody who passed that spot bow to it. That was one of his kinder actions. He confiscated land from the Swiss, robbing them of huge sources of income in rents and tithes, and insulted them. When William Tell refused to bow to the hat, a series of insults between the two men led to Tell having to shoot an apple off his son's head. Tell, who was known for his excellent aim, knocked the apple off with no injury to his child, but told Gessler that his second arrow would have been for him had his son died. This infuriated Gessler, who had Tell arrested. En route to jail, Tell escaped and ambushed Gessler, who got his comeuppance in the form of Tell's spare arrow through the heart. Tell became a national hero and a Swiss symbol of freedom.

Events from the history of Lucerne and the Swiss Confederation are depicted in a series of triangular tableaux between the rafters of the Chapel Bridge in Lucerne.

THE SWISS CONFEDERATION IN THE 15TH CENTURY

The Confederation of eight Swiss states began to look on expansion as their best defense. In the early 15th century, they took more land from the Habsburg Empire, while other Swiss cantons decided to declare their own independence without joining the Confederation. They negotiated a temporary peace with the Habsburgs and instead took land from the Burgundian Empire. In March 1476, a Burgundian army was defeated by a Swiss force at Grandson, and later that year in Morat, both towns in western Switzerland. These wars continued until 1477, and all the while the reputation of the Swiss as soldiers grew. But as the Confederation took more and more land, they began to quarrel among themselves. In 1481, on the verge of civil war, they signed a new pact and drew two new cantons into the Confederation. Now a Confederation of 10 states, they were joined in the next 30 years by three more.

The Confederation began to grow rich, partly on the spoils of the many battles its mercenaries began to undertake on behalf of foreign kingdoms. Although Switzerland today stands for neutrality, for many years there were no major wars in Europe that did not have Swiss soldiers fighting on one side or another. The chief export of Switzerland became soldiers, and as their military prowess grew, so did the wealth of the city cantons. But this was not to last. Other countries learned the lessons of the Swiss mercenaries and set up competing mercenary forces. Warfare underwent a massive change during this century, and the high cost of military equipment began to make the prospect of peace more financially rewarding to European rulers.

THE REFORMATION

At the start of the 16th century things were definitely on a downturn for the Swiss Confederation, which now comprised 13 states and several occupied territories. Their reputation as mercenaries had declined, there was less demand for troops all over Europe, and they had been badly defeated in the battle of Marignano in 1515.

Worse was to come in the form of the Reformation. In the rest of Europe the division between politics and religion was established, and while the Reformation wrought dramatic changes all over the continent, none were affected so thoroughly as Switzerland.

Swiss Protestant reformer Huldreich Zwingli is given a sad but rousing send-off by his supporters as he leaves Zurich.

The Reformation, led by Martin Luther in Germany, was a crusade against what was seen as corrupt practices in the Roman Catholic Church. Chief among these were the way in which the Church involved itself in secular matters, its financial corruption, and the ceremonies and furnishings of the Church itself that had become ostentatious, with the acquisition of paintings, statues, and valuable artifact.

In Switzerland, the reforms were led by Huldreich Zwingli ("OOL-rik TSWING-li"), who saw the religious changes as part of a larger picture, the reform of society, starting in Zurich. He believed that in order to build a new society, it was necessary to destroy the old one. Zurich had long had a very bad reputation, and the city council was pleased to encourage him in his reforms. All decorations were thrown out of the churches, and in 1523, the Catholic rites were abolished in favor of Protestant services. The rural cantons surrounding Zurich did not go along with these changes and issued warrants for Zwingli's arrest. This led to war between the city's forces and the rural cantons in 1531. In the ensuing battle Zwingli was killed.

The "Lion of Lucerne" monument commemorates the heroism of those Swiss guards who were slain while defending the Tuileries Palace in Paris in 1792.

In Geneva, another reformer dominated, a man called John Calvin, who formed his own set of religious beliefs. If more extreme than Zwingli's, they concentrated on the church alone rather than interfering in state affairs. Calvin set up a tribunal of 12 men in Geneva to sit in judgment on religious matters. Anyone who disapproved of the new austere lifestyle of the city left or took the consequences, which were often severe.

The shock waves of the Reformation continued to blast Europe for the next century. Before the end of the Reformation, there was one last destructive convulsion. This was the Thirty Years' War, a series of wars fought by various nations for various reasons, including religious, dynastic, and territorial. During the wars the Swiss Confederation remained neutral, although the basic divisions that had opened up between the Protestant urban cantons and the rural Catholic ones meant that the cantons supported different parties in the wars.

Ironically, as soon as the Thirty Years' War ended in 1648, the Swiss, now acknowledged by the rest of Europe as an independent confederation of states, went to war with itself. The division was again between the Protestant urban cantons and the Catholic rural ones. In addition, many of the lands that the Confederation had taken over through the centuries were beginning to revolt against their heavy taxes.

THE FRENCH INVASION

In 1789, the French Revolution occurred and the vassal Swiss states such as Vaud followed the French example and rose up against their Swiss overlords. French military forces invaded Switzerland in defense of the revolting cantons. For a brief period, Switzerland became a French satellite state. Finally, in 1803, French Emperor Napoleon Bonaparte enforced a

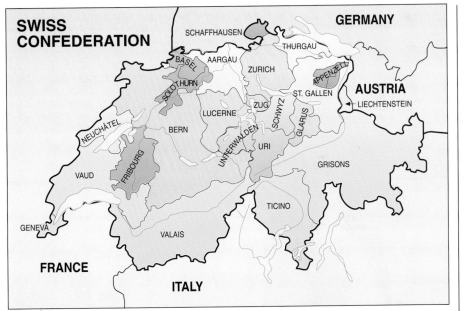

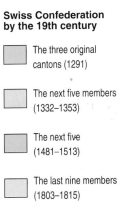

settlement on the Confederation, giving them some sovereignty and making six of the previous vassal states members of the Confederation. In 1815, after more wrangling between the cantons, three more of the vassal states became full members of the Confederation. By now there were 22 cantons in the Confederation. It was during this period, too, that Switzerland's neutrality was recognized internationally.

A NEW CONSTITUTION

From 1830 onward, liberal constitutions were drawn up in 12 cantons. The year 1847 saw the end of a brief civil war between the Catholic cantons that broke off to form a separate government called the Sonderbund and the other Swiss cantons. In 1848, this dispute resulted in the drawing up of a new constitution. A form of government evolved with a federal government in charge of foreign affairs and disputes between states, while the local governments took care of the day-to-day running of each state. The rest of Europe continued in a state of turmoil for much of the 19th century, while the Swiss Confederation had finally found a means of peacefully coexisting, yet remaining neutral in European and world affairs. The last canton to join the Confederation was the Jura in 1979.

The St. Gotthard Pass is an important road and railway route between central Europe and Italy. The 10-mile St. Gotthard Tunnel is one of the longest tunnels in the world.

SWISS NEUTRALITY AND THE TWO WORLD WARS

With many clearly differentiated cultural groups, Switzerland's neutrality and even its existence as an independent state was continually at risk. During the Franco-Prussian War of 1870–1871, German Swiss supported Prussia, while French Swiss supported France. In 1916, the assassination of Archduke Ferdinand, which set in motion a chain of events that resulted in World War I, brought all the French-German tensions back to the forefront of Swiss life. Shortly after the war began, Swiss neutrality was threatened when it was discovered that German sympathizers were passing military secrets to the German side. While Swiss soldiers patrolled the borders, the Swiss economy felt the pinch of the war. Large numbers of refugees fled into Switzerland.

After the war, with its neutrality intact, Switzerland faced the dilemma of whether it could remain neutral and still join the newly formed League of Nations, the predecessor of the United Nations. It became a member in 1920, but when World War II began to take shape, Switzerland was given special dispensation to ignore any trade sanctions against Germany. For the duration of the war, Switzerland traded with both the Allies and the Axis powers. Its borders were patrolled by 850,000 troops, and the Alps became the designated spot where German invading troops would be met and stopped. The St. Gotthard Tunnel, a major artery through the Alps, was permanently mined and was to be the first casualty of any German

invasion. Although German plans for an invasion of Switzerland were discovered, it never took place, and Switzerland emerged from World War II with a booming economy among the ruins of the rest of Europe. It was thus perfectly placed to benefit from the enormous needs of reconstructing Europe. After World War II, Switzerland reverted to complete neutrality by refusing to join the United Nations, since doing so would mean possible involvement in military commitments.

In more recent times, Switzerland has experienced other challenges to its stability. It became one of the last European states to grant women the vote, experienced a huge influx of foreign workers and refugees, and has met the challenges of the growing economies of Japan and Germany. It now faces the serious challenge of entry to the European Community (EC). If Switzerland does not join the EC, it will suffer economic isolation, but if it does join, its neutrality will be compromised. Either way, whether by economic pressures or by the dissolution of its sense of statehood as it accepts more and more regulations determined in Brussels, the EC headquarters, Switzerland's future seems set for a major change.

Formerly the headquarters of the League of Nations, the Palais des Nations in Geneva today houses offices of the United Nations. Although Switzerland did not join the United Nations, it is a member of many international organizations, including the United Nations Educational, Scientific, and Cultural Organization (UNESCO) and the International Labor Organization (ILO).

GOVERNMENT

THE SWISS SYSTEM OF GOVERNMENT today is very much the same as that set up by the country's 1848 Constitution. It has a Federal Assembly consisting of a bicameral legislative body. The two houses are the National Council, similar in function to the U.S. House of Representatives, and the Council of States, similar in function to the Senate. The National Council has 200 members elected for a four-year term by proportional representation, and the Council of States has 46 members selected by the cantons.

An executive body called the Federal Council is elected every four years. It is known abroad as the Cabinet. Every year, a new president of the Federation is chosen from among the members of the Federal Council. The president's job is largely ceremonial.

Each canton is a sovereign state with its own government consisting of an executive and a legislative body. These state governments are responsible for education, public health, police, and local taxes.

Although elections to all these bodies take place every four years, the Swiss voter probably has more selections to make than in any other democracy. Referenda are common occurrences, with voting and elections held on weekends to cause as little disruption as possible.

Opposite: **Parliament Building in Bern where the Federal Assembly convenes four times a year.**

Above: **The Confederation Centre in Geneva. Geneva is the headquarters of many public and private international organizations.**

THE CONSTITUTION

Before 1848, the Swiss Confederation consisted of a loose organization of 25 independent cantons, each with its own system of government, ranging from democracy to oligarchy and aristocracy.

The 1848 Constitution set up a Republican government in the middle of restored European monarchies. It gave control of foreign affairs to the federal government, imposed democratic government on all the cantons, and banned the hiring out of mercenary armies. The Constitution was revised in 1874 and has been adjusted many times by referendum.

A major review of the Constitution began again in 1967, but so far this has not brought about a new constitution.

THE FEDERAL COUNCIL

The highest authority is the Federal Council. Each of its seven members is responsible for a government department—defense, transportation and energy, justice and the police, the economy, finance, foreign affairs, and the interior. Three of the political parties are represented by two seats, while the fourth has one seat. No two members can come from the same canton. In 1984, the first woman was elected to the council.

THE LEGAL SYSTEM

In 1912, the Swiss Civil Code was written and since then many parts of it have been adopted wholesale by other countries setting up their own civil laws. The cantons run their own courts, with those convicted having access to the Federal Court of Appeal. Capital punishment was abolished in 1937 in all the cantons.

Between 1900 and 1950, 100 referenda were held in Switzerland. Between 1950 and 1988, 200 were held, which indicates the increased involvement of the people in deciding the course of government.

CIVIL RIGHTS IN SWITZERLAND

Switzerland is a signatory to the European Convention on Human Rights, and each citizen's rights are laid down by both federal and cantonal law. The Constitution guarantees freedom of property ownership, freedom of trade and commerce, freedom of choice of domicile and worship, freedom of the press, and rights of association and petition. All men (and since 1971, women) aged 20 and over have the right to elect their representatives and to take an active part in deciding on legislation.

The right of initiative enables any citizen to propose a change to the Constitution. If 100,000 electors sign a proposed constitutional change, the federal government can make a counterproposal and a popular vote is taken on the issue.

The citizens also have a right to demand a referendum on any new piece of legislation. If 50,000 electors or eight cantons demand a referendum within 90 days of a new piece of legislation being published, the referendum will be held. If the voters decide against it, the legislation is dropped or altered.

A protest march on a street in Zurich. The Swiss are quite involved with the process of democracy.

THE FEDERAL COURT

The Federal Court is the supreme arbiter of justice in Switzerland and is based at Lausanne. Its function is mainly as a court of appeal on judgments passed by the cantonal courts. Its judgments on cases become the law of the land. Other judges at lower levels must use the Supreme Court's judgments as models for their own. The Federal Court also arbitrates disputes between the cantons.

CANTONS AND STATES

In the chapter on history, the words "canton" and "state" were used as alternatives for the same political unit, but that is not quite right in the modern context. In present-day Switzerland, there are 23 states but 26 cantons. Three of the original cantons were divided up. Unterwalden, one of the three original signatories to the Confederation, was divided in the 12th century into Obwalden and Nidwalden, while Appenzell was divided into Appenzell Outer-Rhodes and Appenzell Inner-Rhodes in 1597, and Basel into Basel-Town and Basel-Country in 1833. Each of the half cantons has its own independent regional government, but only half the voting power of the other full cantons in the federal government.

Within each canton, a government of around seven members is elected. Besides the government, the canton also has a parliament with one chamber. The number of representatives varies with each canton. Parliamentary elections are held on average every four years, again depending on the canton. The parliaments are empowered to collect taxes and decide on matters of education and social services.

At the administrative level below the canton, Switzerland is divided into 3,061 communes, each with its own local authority. Each commune has its own assembly, which anyone can attend to elect authorities or even take part in the running of affairs. The commune is responsible for the upkeep of public property such as forests, water, gas and electrical power, bridges, roads, administrative buildings, fire departments, and many other local services. The size of each commune varies greatly. Some of them are larger than the small cantons; others are tiny. A Swiss individual remains permanently a member of the commune where his or her father was born, but when a woman marries, she joins her husband's commune.

THE LANDSGEMEINDE

The *Landsgemeinde* ("LAHNTS-geh-min-de"), an outdoor assembly of people gathered for the purpose of conducting government business, is an ancient tradition dating back to the 13th century. Once, all the cantons elected their leaders in this way, but now it is only practiced in five of the Swiss cantons. Every spring, usually on the last Sunday in April, the voters of Glarus, Appenzell, and Unterwalden hold an open-air meeting in the main squares of their capital towns to elect their magistrates for the following year. Voting is by a show of hands.

In the half canton of Appenzell (Inner Rhodes), the *Landsgemeinde* consists of around 12,000 people. They gather in the town square of Trogen or Hundwil. The ceremony is opened by the chief magistrate, the *Landammann*. The elections are held and then the newly sworn-in magistrates take an oath to be faithful to the people and vow faithfulness to the *Landammann*. This is followed by prayers and hymns.

Landsgemeinde, the constitutional assembly of free citizens, is held in the open in the canton of Glarus.

POLITICAL PARTIES

A two-party political system, such as is found in the United States, does not exist in Switzerland. We have seen that as a matter of custom each party is represented on the Federal Council so no one political group can really dominate or determine policy. There are around 11 different parties represented in the National Council, ranging from the larger groups such as Christian Democrats, Radical Democrats, Social Democrats, and Swiss People's Party right down to environmentalist groups and independents. The fact that the parties are able to cooperate so easily in government shows that they have very few major differences.

In addition to this type of political grouping, the system allows for pressure groups to form. Because of the citizens' rights to call for a referendum on national issues, groups form continuously in order to force discussion on certain topics. Conservationists, the anti-nuclear lobby, anti-fascist groups, and anti-abortion groups have all used their rights to call for a referendum on the issues they think are important.

FOREIGN POLICY

Switzerland long ago came to realize that, surrounded as it was by potential aggressors, its safest form of defense was neutrality. Switzerland's neutrality was accepted in the 1815 Congress of Vienna and the 1919 Treaty of Versailles. But neutrality is not an easy position to hold in a world where increasingly countries are forming alliances in order to survive. Switzerland cannot enter any international agreement that might oblige the country to come to another's aid. It is not a part of NATO or the United Nations. Even now, Switzerland is not yet a part of the European Community. This is as much because of its own need to protect its home industries as well as its political need to remain neutral.

Although Switzerland does not take sides in international disputes, the country puts a great deal of effort into its foreign policy. Switzerland spends huge sums on international aid to developing countries and has a relief corps that is dispatched to any natural disaster. Switzerland maintains political relations with as many countries as possible and often acts as a go-between or mediator between countries that have cut off political relations with one another but still need to communicate.

In addition, Geneva is home to many international organizations that are involved in human rights and humanitarian international law.

Over the years, many people have criticized Switzerland's stance on neutrality, which has often proved to be lucrative. While their neighbors were at war, Switzerland has traded with both sides. It has been said too that Switzerland's banks have provided safekeeping for many people with their ill-gotten gains. But Switzerland provides an international service via the International Red Cross, maintaining a fleet of aircraft to be dispatched anywhere in the world where there are war casualties. During World War II, Switzerland opened its borders to 300,000 refugees.

Swiss army tanks patrol the streets. The Swiss army is a militia, that is, it is made up of citizen soldiers rather than professional ones.

THE ARMED FORCES

To protect their neutrality, the Swiss make sure they can defend the country against invasion. To this end, all able-bodied men between the ages of 20 and 50 are permanently on call for national service. All men undergo a basic training program, followed by eight years of supplementary annual training, and in the case of officers, further training courses until age 50 or 55.

Women who are interested join the Auxiliary Force. In addition, huge amounts of money have been spent providing the population with underground shelters in case of nuclear war between Switzerland's neighbors. Each man keeps his own weapons at home, ready for action. In 1939, when war broke out, the Swiss Army was mobilized and the borders were protected even before the war was announced in the British Parliament. During the battle of France in 1940, Germany violated Switzerland's neutrality by sending warplanes into Swiss airspace. They were shot down and the incursions stopped.

ECONOMY

CONSIDERING THAT IT has massive disadvantages in terms of raw materials, transportation, land, and even population, Switzerland has done remarkably well over the years. It has one of the highest standards of living of any Western country, and the largest per capita export market. From the Middle Ages onwards, Switzerland's chief export was a group of well-trained soldiers who would fight for whichever king paid them the most. Back in the Middle Ages, Switzerland grew rich on the spoils of war. After the battles of Grandson and Morat in 1476, when the Swiss routed the Burgundian armies, huge hauls of booty were taken that included enormous diamonds, silks, and plain hard cash. Swiss neutrality in later years ensured that these resources were never lost.

During the Thirty Years' War in the 17th century, the Swiss grew rich on trading with the belligerents, supplying cereals, vegetables, and meat to countries so war-torn that they could not grow their own food. Switzerland also took in refugees whose skills began the Swiss tradition of producing tiny intricate objects such as watches and jewels.

Nowadays Switzerland has thriving banking, watchmaking, chocolate, chemical, and pharmaceutical industries, as well as a burgeoning tourist trade.

Opposite: **Switzerland's political and monetary stability, its neutrality, and its special banking system have made it one of the world's most important financial centers. Banks such as this Swiss National Bank contribute their expertise to Switzerland's unique financial system.**

Above: **Swiss chocolates are world-renowned. Chocolate factories such as this one make hundreds of varieties of chocolate, in all shapes and sizes.**

Agriculture in Switzerland is characterized by fodder crops and grazing. Cattle, horses, pigs, and sheep are raised, and dairy products are important to the economy.

AGRICULTURE

Two-thirds of Switzerland's landmass is rock, water, or forest. Urban growth uses up another large chunk of the potential agricultural land so that only one quarter of the total land surface is suitable for agriculture.

The number of people involved in agricultural production has declined rapidly. In the 19th century, 60% of the population worked in agriculture. By World War II, this had dropped to 22%, and it is now less than 6%. This does not mean, however, that agricultural production has dropped. Farms are now much larger than they once were and are highly mechanized.

In the mountain regions, the chief activity is raising livestock, mostly cattle. In the central plateau and lower Alpine valleys, grapevines, vegetables, and tobacco are grown in addition to livestock. Livestock accounts for four-fifths of agricultural production, while milk production is at a surplus. Cheese and chocolate, both milk products, are exported, but few other foods are. Swiss vineyards produce about half the country's needs. Grapes are grown in Ticino, the valleys of the Rhone, and the south-facing slopes above Lake Geneva, Lake Neuchâtel, Lake Biel, and Lake Zurich.

Many agricultural products are protected by the government against cheaper imports by means of customs duties on imports and fixed prices paid to farmers for grain, milk, and sugar beets. This need to protect the domestic agricultural industry is one of the chief reasons Switzerland has been reluctant to be a part of the European Community.

MACHINERY AND ELECTRONICS

The machine, electronics, and metallurgical industries account for 45% of Switzerland's total exports. Almost half the total workforce is employed in these industries. The Swiss machine industry includes everything from machine tools and precision instruments to heavy electrical equipment. The machine tool industry originally developed out of the needs of Switzerland's own textile industry, which peaked during the 19th century. The development of railways, hydroelectric power, and the motorization of seagoing vessels all called for complex machinery, which was developed in Switzerland. The Swiss built the first electric track railway, the first turbo-generator, the first pump turbine, and the first gas turbine power station. As electronics have become more important in industry, Swiss technology has kept pace.

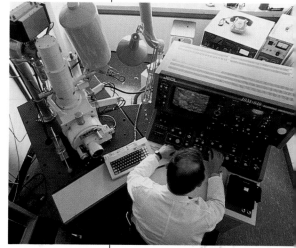

Switzerland's industries have gone high-tech. Industries employ electronics to produce a wide range of quality products and services.

CHEMICALS AND PHARMACEUTICALS

The Swiss chemical industry, like the machine tool industry, developed out of the needs of the textile factories of the 19th century. Dyes were needed for the woven cloth and so the dyestuff industry developed. Today, dyes are made for cloth, leather, paper, paints, and varnishes.

The pharmaceutical industry is very capital-intensive. Each new drug takes at least 12 years of research and testing before it can be put on the market. Ciba Geigy, Hoffman La Roche, and Sandoz are all Swiss-based pharmaceutical firms with research and processing plants all over the world.

Top and bottom: **A Swiss watch factory, and Swatch watches on display. Switzerland's watch industry produces everything from chronometers to quartz and mechanical watches—all with the same exacting Swiss precision and accuracy.**

THE WATCH INDUSTRY

French refugees of the 16th century first brought skills to Switzerland that made possible the development of the watch industry. The first watchmakers' guild in Switzerland was established in the 17th century in Geneva. From there the industry spread out along the Jura Mountains to Schaffhausen. Mass production of tiny parts began in Switzerland in 1845, long before other countries had the technology, so Switzerland gained an enormous advantage over other watchmaking areas. Nowadays, over 70 million watches and moving parts are manufactured in Switzerland and the bulk of them are exported to other countries.

In 1921, the Swiss Laboratory of Horological Research was set up so Swiss manufacturers could pool ideas. In the 1960s, the first quartz watch was manufactured in Switzerland. Liquid crystal displays (LCDs), electro-chromic displays, combined analog and digital displays, and optic sensors were all developed in Switzerland. The most recent inventions are a watch that is 0.98 millimeters thick and a human voice-responsive watch.

After the 1970s, the whole industry was reorganized to meet the increasing competition from Japan's inexpensive quartz watches. Switzerland has learned to compete effectively in this area, where price is an important factor. However, it still dominates the world markets in expensive watches with handmade mechanical parts.

TEXTILES

Fabric and lace are two of the oldest manufactured goods in Switzerland. The textile industry dates back to the Middle Ages when spinning and weaving were the dominant professions in certain towns. Silk was associated with Zurich, drapery with Fribourg, and linen and cotton with St. Gallen. These were cottage industries, with small home workshops producing materials for the towns' buyers. Even now, textile companies are small compared to other industries and are still decentralized.

The textile industry is dependent on a good export market and is susceptible to economic downturns in other countries. After World War II, for example, the embroidery industry, which had employed 100,000 people in the northeast cantons, was virtually wiped out. But the industry has regained some of its former strength by developing mass production methods. Automation has replaced the skilled worker. Today, 60% of textile products are exported.

A wool-processing plant in operation. The textile industry is the oldest in Switzerland, dating back to the 13th century. Automation has led to restructuring, and today Switzerland is one of the main exporters of machinery and equipment for the textile industry.

Switzerland's scenic landscape and excellent tourist facilities make it an ideal vacation spot throughout the year. Resort chalets such as this cater to the many tourists who vacation in Switzerland annually, including a large number of Swiss.

TOURISM

Switzerland may well have been the first tourist destination in the world. It has been a magnet for tourists since 1787, when Horace Saussure published an ode to the Alps, praising their beauty and interest. Switzerland has clean air, beautiful scenery, winter and other sports, lots of history, and plenty of culture. More than 11 million foreign tourists visit the country every year.

Tourism accounts for one of the largest workforces in the country. In 1990, Switzerland earned 15 billion francs from tourism, making it the third biggest earner after machinery and chemicals. Unlike other countries in Western Europe, tourism in Switzerland is not limited to the summer season. Winter offers skiing, sledding, tobogganing, and ice-skating, while summer brings golf, boating, walking, and climbing, as well as the usual tourist interests. The major winter resorts are St. Moritz, Gstaad, and Interlaken.

Tourism has had a beneficial effect on the country in ways other than national income. Regions that might have become depopulated have developed as tourist areas; chalets and cottages that might have fallen into ruin have become holiday homes.

But there are drawbacks. Demand for new ski resorts and hotels have made claims on an already shrinking countryside. Laws have been introduced to control the design of the new resorts and to protect endangered plants. Visitors are now encouraged to visit during the less busy seasons—spring and fall.

BANKING

Perhaps Switzerland's most famous industry is banking. The idea of saving for the future is deeply rooted in Swiss society and has given rise to a unique financial network. Switzerland has over 4,000 branches of banks and other financial institutions. Many foreign investors use Swiss banks, attracted largely by laws regarding secrecy, but also by the stability of Swiss society. Investors can make use of numbered bank accounts, whose ownership is known only to a tiny number of people. However, if criminal activity is suspected, the bank's respect for the secrecy of its client can be dismissed. The net profit of all Swiss banks in 1989 was 5.9 billion francs.

Information on stocks and shares is monitored on the floor of the Zurich Stock Exchange via an efficient computer network system.

FOREIGN WORKERS

Switzerland has a higher proportion of foreign residents than any other European country. For many years the rate of increase of the Swiss population has not kept up with the needs of industry and so workers from other countries, chiefly neighboring European ones, have come to live in the country. Guest workers from Italy, Spain, and Portugal provide the low-paid manual labor needed to construct some of Switzerland's major infrastructure projects, such as highways.

Switzerland has benefited a great deal in the past from the influx of foreign workers and refugees from European wars. The official figures for foreign workers are actually lower than the real ones since there are many people living near the Swiss borders who commute into Switzerland for work. Many seasonal workers, too, move to tourist areas such as Lugano just for one season before returning to Italy or Spain.

THE SWISS

FORMED BY PEOPLE of different ethnicity and language, the Swiss have found a unique way to coexist and maintain their diversity. Switzerland's federalism incorporates an enormous respect for the cultural differences of its people and a determination to preserve those differences. If a nation can be said to have certain characteristics, the Swiss are conservative, unfussy, prudent, and industrious.

Switzerland stands at a crossroads where several cultures meet, with France to the west, Germany to the north, and Italy to the south. In addition, a relic group exists within the heart of Switzerland that speaks a language derived from a mixture of Latin and an older language now lost. Switzerland also has different religions. Catholics and Protestants live side by side in almost equal numbers, and there is a tiny Jewish community.

Switzerland has a population of about 6.7 million. Of this number, over a million are foreign workers.

Opposite: **An Appenzell herdsman in striking red and yellow apparel talks to a cattle dealer.**

Below: **Two elderly Swiss gentlemen engage in deep conversation.**

Sixty percent of the total population of Switzerland lives in urban areas.

47

A family vineyard near Mendrisio in the southern canton of Ticino. Wine is produced in large quantities in the vineyards of this region.

THE PEOPLE OF TICINO

Ticino is the part of Switzerland that is closest to Italy. At various times in Switzerland's history it was annexed by Italy. Most of its people speak Italian, and are Mediterranean in complexion and character.

Ticino is a mountainous and fairly inhospitable canton. Summers are often marked by severe thunderstorms that cause the Ticino River to flood much of the arable land. It has traditionally been quite a depressed area economically, and in the early years of this century over 25,000 of its inhabitants emigrated. Very little of the region is actually flat arable land, and the typical Ticino home is a stone-roofed cottage high in the hills. Until recently the people were largely farmers, growing tobacco in the Mendrisio area and grapevines and olives on the slopes above the lakes.

The lifestyle of the Ticino people has been affected greatly by the rising interest in tourism in the area and the increasing wealth of the other cantons. Many of the old stone-roofed cottages high in the mountains have been purchased as summer homes for the wealthy residents of Zurich. In fact, every fourth home in Ticino is a vacation home. At the same time, many of the local inhabitants have emigrated to the other more prosperous cantons to work.

But there have been improvements in the lives of the people of this canton. Ticino has become a center of tourism and international finance, and particularly in the city of Lugano, many people have found work in the service industries located around the new highways in the canton.

THE PEOPLE OF THE GRISONS

The origins of the people who live in this upland region of Switzerland are lost in the mists of time. The people living here are believed to be of a completely different origin than those of French and German heritage, and their language is thought to have evolved from different sources.

Most Europeans are believed to be of Indo-European origin, but not so the people of the Grisons. Their Romansh language has Etruscan, Semitic, and perhaps Celtic influences on top of the basic Latin imposed by the Romans. The area held out against the Romans for 40 years after the rest of Switzerland was conquered in 58 B.C. As the Roman Empire gave way to invasions from Germanic tribes in the fifth century, the Rhaetians, who were the original settlers, regained their independence. The Burgundian wars followed, and for a time the region was a subject state. Next came domination by the Habsburgs, until the Rhaetians formed the League of the House of God to defend themselves against further encroachments by foreign powers.

Today, the Grisons is Switzerland's largest canton, occupying about one-sixth of the country, around 2,800 square miles. Although it also contains Swiss German and Italian speakers, it is characterized by the Romansh language spoken by about a third of its population. The Grisons is largely rural, and many of the people find employment in the very exclusive winter resorts in the area. In all, there are about a hundred resorts in this region.

Horse-drawn sleighs provide a means of transportation for the people of the Grisons. One of the most picturesque spots, the Grisons is an important tourist destination and the tourist industry provides jobs for many of its inhabitants.

49

IMMIGRANTS

For centuries foreigners have come to Switzerland as a place of refuge. Some very famous people have made Switzerland their home, however temporarily. Lenin lived in Switzerland for a time, as did James Joyce and the 19th-century German writers, Goethe and Schiller. Mary Shelley wrote her novel *Frankenstein* in Switzerland. Richard Wagner, the German composer, left his native Germany and took refuge in Switzerland. Freidrich Nietzsche, who taught at Basel University, got the ideas for his work *Thus Spake Zarathustra* while on vacation in the Engadine, in the Grisons. Einstein, escaping from Nazi Germany, did much of his work on the theory of relativity in Switzerland. Bertolt Brecht, Igor Stravinsky, and Leon Trotsky all found Switzerland a safe place to await their moment of fame.

Many famous people still find their way to Switzerland, attracted by the banking system and the tax concessions. However, the new immigrants to Switzerland are the large numbers of foreign workers attracted by the good wages and escape from difficult political situations in their home countries. In 1990, there were 1,100,000 foreigners living in Switzerland, making up 16.4% of the population. Many refugees have also added to the total number of foreigners.

THE PEOPLE OF THE VALAIS

The Valais was a late entrant into the Confederation, joining in 1815 after centuries of exploitation by the French dukes of Savoy and eventually Napoleon's France. For Valais, joining the Confederation was a last resort rather than an achievement.

The Valais is a narrow valley, 80 miles long, lying between the Valaisian and Bernese Alps, and the skylines are dominated by mountain horizons. Running off from the central valley are many smaller valleys that even today are quite inaccessible.

The people of the Valais have always seen themselves as a race apart from the rest of Switzerland and, if a whole group of people can be characterized, would probably describe themselves as headstrong, self-confident, and very independent. They are largely French-speaking and have a very distinctive accent that any Swiss can recognize after hearing the first few words. In some rural areas a dialect of French is spoken.

Traditional lifestyles here have been dominated by the climate. Each spring the animals are taken up to the summer pastures high on the mountains, to be brought back down again in the fall.

Opposite: **With its pleasant summer temperatures and some 50 peaks, most notably the Matterhorn, the Valais has become an important resort area.**

EMIGRANTS

During Switzerland's period of industrialization, many people chose to leave the country in search of a new agricultural life rather than make the move to the cities to work. The United States and Australia were major destinations for the poor Swiss farmers.

In the more distant past, the Swiss left their home country to work as mercenaries in foreign armies. Nowadays, the majority of Swiss who leave their country are professionals going abroad for experience or to promote some Swiss industry. About 456,000 Swiss people live abroad, 127,000 of them in North and South America.

COSTUMES

There are almost as many different traditional costumes in Switzerland as there are valleys. These costumes are highly regarded and valued, and are worn during the many festive occasions in Switzerland. Many of them display the Swiss craft of embroidery.

The most distinctive ones are probably those of the Gruyère region. The *armailli* or herdsman of the Gruyère wears the *bredzon,* a short blue cloth or canvas jacket with the sleeves gathered at the shoulders, embroidered with edelweiss at the lapels. The woman's dress from the same region is plain and worn with a red scarf round the neck. For festivals, she wears a silk apron and a long-sleeved jacket. The straw hat is edged with velvet and has crocheted ribbons hanging down.

Women from St. Gallen wear shimmering gold lace caps, while women from Appenzell wear lace caps with spreading wings. The Appenzell herdsman wears intricate

trousers with heavily-patterned straps, and suspenders carrying pictures of the cows he tends. He wears a silver earring in his right ear. In Unterwalden, the woman's dress is very ornate with silver ornaments, and a silver comb is worn in the side of the hair. The man's shirt from the same region is heavily embroidered.

LIFESTYLE

SWITZERLAND ENJOYS A PRIVILEGED POSITION in the world. This is due, among other things, to its early industrialization and a well-educated population that has enabled the country to specialize in producing high-quality products and providing valuable services. Peopled by diverse ethnic and linguistic groups, the nation has learned to survive as a cohesive unit.

There is no doubt that the Swiss are conscious of both their own wealth and their exemption from the major buffets of fate. However, more than just being a collection of bank managers, clockmakers, and chocolate entrepreneurs, Switzerland has led the world in other important ways, such as in its long tradition of aid and disaster relief work.

Opposite: **A boy poses beside his bicycle. Cycling is a popular activity enjoyed by young and old.**

Below: **A wooden farmhouse in Switzerland offers a picturesque and tranquil scene. Here, a Swiss mother takes time off from her chores to play with her child.**

Like most main cities in Switzerland, Lausanne, the capital of Vaud, is densely populated.

LIFE IN THE CITIES

The cities and towns of Switzerland are home to more than 60% of the population. Each city has its own character, determined by its population makeup, its function as a city, and its architectural heritage. As in other world cities, urban growth and the demand for inner city office buildings have meant that large suburban areas have grown up around the cities. Swiss cities are quite heavily populated, and commuters on their way to work may spend time waiting in line for buses, the metro, or the ferryboat.

Swiss people have the longest working hours in all of Europe. The work day begins early—most businesses and banks are open by 8 a.m.—and ends at around 5 p.m.

In the cities, sidewalk cafés are one of the focal points of daily life. In summer, they are crowded with workers and tourists having their lunch or watching the world go by. In the French-speaking cities, the people prefer to drink wine with their lunch, while in the German-speaking towns such as Zurich, beer is the more popular choice.

Nightlife in the cities begins early, at around 8 p.m. For those who want a night out there is sufficient entertainment to keep them occupied, from restaurants and movie theaters to clubs and bars. The evening's activities end as early as they begin. By midnight, the restaurants and bars are closed and only the most avant-garde of clubs stay open until 2 or 3 a.m.

Swiss cities are prone to almost as many problems as cities in other countries. In Zurich and other major cities, drugs are a real problem, with some city parks becoming centers for young drug users who have dropped out of mainstream society. Many cantons give free syringes to drug users in an attempt to combat AIDS. Increasingly, Swiss cities are experiencing the mugging and petty theft that accompany a drug culture.

If Swiss city dwellers historically were frugal with their money and worked long hours, they tend to become increasingly less so. They spend more money than in the past and give more thought to leisure and less to the Puritan work ethic. They are also perhaps a lot less sure of their identity. Switzerland is on the verge of joining the European Community. The urban Swiss realize their future lies as part of a united Europe, but fear that their centuries-long neutrality and decentralized democracy will be at stake if they join the EC.

Sidewalk cafés are frequented by Swiss and tourists, who enjoy the alfresco atmosphere.

LIFE IN THE COUNTRY

Around 40% of the population of Switzerland lives in rural areas, but only about 6% is actually engaged in farming. Over the last century, the urbanization of the country has seen large population movements from the country into the cities. At the same time, agricultural output has increased by means of mechanization, improved fertilizers, and economies of scale as farms get much larger.

People in the rural cantons of Switzerland have historically been more conservative in their outlook than those living in the cities. Now many of them find work in the tourism industry, which in Switzerland employs them more or less all year round. Their work day is determined by the same work ethic employed in cities. Hotels must be cleaned and the guests catered to, restaurants must provide the tourists with meals, and sports centers and health spas must be kept in efficient running condition.

For the 6% of Swiss still engaged in farming, life may undergo a drastic change. Switzerland has long protected its farmers from foreign competition, but if it joins the EC, the high tariffs against imports will stop, along with the subsidies for Swiss farms in the form of fixed prices for their products. The government's protection of the farmers is understandable. Their quaint farms and mountain pastures that attract many tourists would become rundown if the tiny rural population

A farmer enlists the help of his family on their farm in Vaud. As more and more farm workers choose other occupations, farming has become increasingly mechanized.

moved away to the cities to find more rewarding work.

In Alpine regions such as the Valais, people live in tiny communities that are continually shrinking. As more and more young people emigrate to the cities, life becomes harder for those left behind, especially since tourism and the desire for country homes has put the price of houses in the countryside out of reach for any poorer person who wishes to live there. The large number of vacation homes also ensures that the winter months are lonely ones for those who live in the country all year round. If the winters are hard and lonely for people in the country, spring and summer bring lots of visitors and festivals to liven up their days.

Guarda, a village in the Engadine of the Grisons. Many village homes such as these have been purchased as summer residences by wealthy Swiss from the urban areas.

LIFE'S MAJOR EVENTS

The majority of the people of Switzerland are practicing Christians, with slightly more Protestants than Catholics. There are also several tiny Jewish communities spread throughout the country. Like other peoples, the Swiss celebrate the major events in a person's life—birth, entry to the church, marriage, retirement, and death.

Children in Davos, in the canton of the Grisons. Swiss children are taught at an early age to respect the virtues of hard work and enterprise.

Birth is celebrated in a quiet ceremony with the family attending church for the baptism. The child's name is decided as a matter of personal taste rather than on any religious grounds. In church, the child is given godparents, who promise to be responsible for the child's religious upbringing. In most cases this is symbolic, although the parents usually choose a close family member or friend.

At the age of 7, the Catholic child receives instruction on the meaning of the Holy Communion, and then in a public ceremony receives the Host with other children of the same age. At 13, both Protestant and Catholic children are confirmed in their religion. Catholic children take a new name at this stage, although it is one they rarely use.

Marriage is still popular in Switzerland, although there are many young people who choose not to observe this ceremony. A church wedding is often followed by a honeymoon abroad. Nowadays many people marry in a civil ceremony.

Swiss funerals are quiet affairs; the family attends a funeral service in church, followed by the burial in the graveyard.

Besides these major events in life, the Swiss observe

other cycles. The change in seasons is celebrated each year, especially in rural areas such as the Valais. There, the farmers wait for spring to come so that they can go with the animals to the high pastures, gradually working their way back down the mountain as the grass is eaten. Celebrations take place during this period, with festivals and mock battles between the cows.

The events of the Christian year are also celebrated in much the same way as in other Christian countries. Religious celebrations, both somber and joyous, are observed in accordance with the Christian calendar, the most important ones being Christmas, Easter, and Corpus Christi.

A well-tended Swiss cemetery. The majority of the Swiss population are either Roman Catholics or Protestants.

A Swiss family gets together for a meal. The Swiss have strong family ties and often go out on social outings together.

SOCIAL INTERACTION

The Swiss are great consumers of the media. Most cities are connected to cable television and so there are many programs to watch. Swiss are also avid newspaper readers. Swiss social life revolves around these things and the family. Nightlife, as we have seen, only extends into the early evening. People work hard—a 42-hour work week is normal—and at the end of a long day, they go home to their families. The coffee shops and bars in the cities and villages are meeting places where people can discuss politics or just read their newspapers in companionable silence.

In a society made up of four distinct language groups, at least three religious groups, and many foreigners, the ability to get along with one's neighbors is a desirable quality that has been bred into the Swiss as a way of life. The Swiss are essentially home-loving, careful people, with a high degree of tolerance, great interest in preserving their cultural heritage, and a great sense of civic duty. They appreciate the benefits of their country's neutrality and the wealth that a public-spirited workforce can bring. There are very few strikes among workers in Switzerland. The Swiss have learned that all differences can be negotiated rather than fought out in public. Since 1937, there has been a regularly renewed agreement between employers and workers to settle their disputes peacefully.

THE ROLE OF WOMEN

Switzerland is by its own admission a conservative country. In a country that values democracy so highly, it is strange that women did not get the right to vote in federal elections until 1971. Women seem not to have minded. This is perhaps because women and men jointly made the decision about voting patterns within their household, although only the men could actually register their vote.

In 1983, Swiss women who marry foreign men were accorded the same rights and privileges as those given to Swiss men who marry foreign women.

Mother and child. Many Swiss women give up their jobs once they start a family. Their daily lives are centered around the family, its problems, and its development.

Women now have the right to equal pay since 1981, although they are still underrepresented in many areas, particularly in politics. In 1984, a woman was elected to the seven-person Federal Council, but she resigned before her term of office ended over a political scandal of which she was later cleared. In 1993, women's voices began to be heard over the issue of women in the Federal Council. Christine Brunner campaigned for a seat on the Federal Council and was about to win it when a smear campaign was directed against her, claiming that she had had an abortion—an illegal act in Switzerland—and that nude photographs of her existed. Ms. Brunner laughed at the stories of nudity, but refused to speak about abortion since she said that it could easily lead to other women being persecuted for what was essentially a matter of conscience. Demonstrations followed the decision to deny her a seat on the council. Ms. Brunner is a lawyer and the leader of one of Switzerland's trade unions.

There are eight universities in Switzerland, four of them in French-speaking areas and four in German-speaking areas. The universities are paid for by the cantons, with the aid of government subsidies.

SOCIAL STRUCTURES

Switzerland is a welfare state, meaning that as part of its duties the state provides all its citizens with free health care, pensions, maternity benefits, and education. These benefits are paid for on the federal level using money that workers contribute to a compulsory national insurance fund, from which they can draw upon in their old age or when sick. At the cantonal level, each canton provides funds and services to the destitute or needy. At the commune level, additional funds are allowed for individual needs. This explains why every Swiss resident must be a member of a commune, and remains a member of that commune unless he or she applies to join another. It is ultimately the responsibility of the commune to look after its needy.

EDUCATION

In Switzerland, each canton is responsible for drawing up its own curriculum, school materials, and teacher-training program for primary, middle, and advanced school education. There are 26 different educational systems operating in Switzerland, one in each canton. The cantons must meet federal standards, but beyond that each canton is autonomous.

Federal regulations determine that schooling starts at age 6 or 7 and continues for eight years. In some cantons, an optional ninth year has been introduced, and all the cantons offer two optional preschool years of kindergarten. Ninety-eight percent of preschool children attend kindergarten for one year; 75% attend for two years. After that, there are between four to six years of primary school, depending on the canton, and three to five years of secondary school. Thus in some cantons, children go to secondary school at age 10, while in others, they move to secondary school at 12.

VOCATIONAL TRAINING

Vocational training, whether undertaken at secondary school level or as part of a higher education program, is conducted in collaboration with private companies. Each canton arranges the training of apprentices. Students study part-time and spend a large proportion of their day in the work-place learning their trade.

Higher vocational training in colleges trains students to become engineers, managers, economists, or social workers.

At the secondary level, children are streamed; that is, they are put into different schools depending on their ability. One category of secondary school offers four years of apprenticeship training leading to a craft or trade of some kind; another offers vocational training; while the third offers academic education, where children are prepared for university or an institute of technology.

This system has its drawbacks, since at the time they enter secondary school children are still young and either do not always know what they want or have not yet reached their full potential. The system is being reviewed so that streaming is delayed, to give young people more time to develop and to obtain a better rounded education.

A classroom lesson in progress. The literacy rate in Switzerland is virtually 100%.

It has been estimated that neutral Switzerland has more weapons per square mile than any other nation in Europe.

NATIONAL DEFENSE

For a neutral country, Switzerland spends a great deal of money on national defense—around the same amount it spends on social welfare. Switzerland has only 3,500 full-time professional soldiers, and the state considers that each man's military obligation is just as important as his civil ones. Thus part of every Swiss man's life is devoted to his military duties.

At the age of 20, the men attend a 17-week training session where they learn the basics and are given their equipment. This equipment, comprising weapons, ammunition, gas mask, and uniform, stays with them at home and they are responsible for maintaining it. Between the ages of 20 and 32, the men attend eight three-week retraining courses. Between the ages of 33 and 42, they are put in the military reserve and attend three two-week courses. After 43, they are still reserve soldiers, but are not obliged to do any more training. In total, all the training in a man's life adds up to about a year. After age 50, the men are usually assigned to civil defense duties.

Once mobilized, the Swiss army would have available 625,000 men and women, military hardware consisting of 800 tanks, 300 jet fighters, and thousands of cannons and missiles. In addition, there are hundreds of camouflaged underground storage caverns and military bases, all of them designed to withstand nuclear blasts.

Other underground storage spaces hold medicine, repair shops for military

Bicycle troops are an essential element of the Swiss army. In the small and often difficult Swiss terrain, they can be faster and more flexible than motorized troops.

THE RED CROSS

If Switzerland has not taken sides in any major European war in the last 400 or 500 years, it has also not turned its back on the suffering of those engaged in those wars. It has become part of the lifestyle of the Swiss, and perhaps part of the justification for their neutrality, to look after those in need. Switzerland is the home and birthplace of the International Red Cross. It was an eccentric Swiss who started the Swiss movement to set up the organization.

Henri Dunant had no intention of being a world benefactor. He was as interested as any other Swiss in setting up a business for himself, and to that end he went to Algeria, where he set up grain mills and began to trade in grain. But things went wrong. The money he borrowed in Switzerland to set up his operation could not be repaid, and so he decided to enlist help from Napoleon III. He followed Napoleon to the battle of Solferino, where he accidentally witnessed the terrible casualties that the battle caused. He spent two days personally helping the injured, and then returned to Switzerland with a lot more on his mind than grain. He toured Switzerland talking about what he had witnessed, and his actions brought about the signing of the first Geneva Convention. Dunant became a public hero for a while, until his creditors caught up with him and he went into hiding, living in poverty in a country village. He got his reward when he received the Nobel Peace prize in 1901—the very first one. Today, the headquarters of the International Red Cross is situated in Geneva and is staffed by Swiss citizens. Switzerland is the guardian of the four Geneva Conventions regarding prisoners of war, the wounded, and refugees.

machinery, and food. For the civilians, there are also underground shelters capable of withstanding heavy bombing. Each year Switzerland builds 200,000 new shelter units, so that by the year 2000, the whole population will have shelter if necessary.

Every new building must include a shelter in its plans. Shelters are built under schools, shopping centers, banks, and even churches. A system of early warning sirens is set up around every canton.

Above: **The headquarters of the International Red Cross in Geneva.**

RELIGION

CHRISTIANITY FIRST CAME to Switzerland through the Roman merchants and soldiers, but it was not until the Middle Ages, quite late in the history of Christianity, that the bulk of the Swiss population was converted. This final conversion was due to the work of a group of traveling Irish missionary monks, led by Columban, an Irish monk. They founded an ancient Celtic religion in Switzerland and hurled into the lakes the graven images of the pagan religion they found there.

In the 16th century, a Catholic Switzerland was racked by the Reformation, when the new Protestants tried to take political power in Zurich. This led to war between the Protestant and the Catholic states. Switzerland, like the rest of Europe, was divided along religious lines. Those divisions again became inflamed in the 19th century, when Lucerne, a predominantly Catholic canton, decided to put its school system under the control of the Jesuits. Protestant groups attacked the city, and the seven Catholic cantons (Lucerne, Uri, Schwyz, Unterwalden, Zug, Fribourg, and Valais) decided to secede from the Confederation. The civil war that followed, known as the Sonderbund War, lasted 20 days and about 100 people were killed. The dispute led to the Swiss Constitution of 1848, which among other things, declared complete religious tolerance, with the exception of the Jesuits, who were banned from Switzerland.

Opposite: **The interior of a church in Lucerne, a predominantly Catholic canton.**

Above: **A village church in Gsteig, in southwest Switzerland.**

69

The 1874
Constitution
guaranteed full
religious liberty,
but repeated
the 1848
Constitution's
prohibition of
settlement by
Jesuits and their
affiliated societies
in Switzerland.
This anti-Jesuit
article was
repealed in a
national
referendum in
1973.

The importance of religious tolerance has remained to this day. The once clear divisions of cantons into Catholic and Protestant camps has softened since the Industrial Revolution, when large numbers of people from the rural cantons moved to the cities. Now 15 cantons have a Catholic majority, while 11 are chiefly Protestant. The Catholic areas are mainly the southern Italian-speaking ones as well as those in central Switzerland. The French-speaking areas, and the areas to the north and east, are largely Protestant. Nationally, about 44% are Protestant, while 47% are Catholic. Jews make up about 0.3% of the population, and the unaffiliated and other religions make up the rest.

PROTESTANTISM

Almost half the population of Switzerland are Protestants. During the Reformation, the two main centers of Protestantism were Zurich, under the influence of Zwingli, and Geneva, under the influence of Calvin. Zurich was and is mostly German-speaking, while Geneva was and is largely French-speaking. Later, Vaud, the canton north of Geneva, and Neuchâtel, its neighbor, were converted. Bern, the largest canton in central Switzerland, also joined the Reformation. As time passed and the citizens of the cantons moved about within the Federation, each city developed a character of its own but had a mixed community of Protestants and Catholics. The various Protestant groups, and there were many of them, formed the Federation of Swiss Evangelical Churches.

In its early stages, Swiss Protestantism was a fiercely puritan religion, disapproving of all frivolity and excess. This can still be seen in the Protestant churches of Switzerland, which are austere and bare compared to the Catholic churches with their highly elaborate artwork and artifacts.

Calvinism, the basis of modern Swiss Protestantism, began as a rejection of some of the tenets of the Church of Rome. It rejected the role of the Pope as God's representative and instead declared that all people could petition directly to God. It refused to accept any doctrine beyond those laid down in the Bible, so that the belief in transubstantiation (the changing of the bread and wine into the body and blood of Christ) was rejected. The ornate decoration of the older churches was thrown out, as was much of the ceremony. More importantly, perhaps, they believed in predestination—the idea that a soul's eventual resting place in heaven or hell is determined before its life even begins.

Today, Protestant churches are managed in each canton by a synod, a body of laymen and laywomen who decide on church matters. Swiss Protestants celebrate the same religious events as Catholics. Christmas, Easter, and Lent figure largely in their religious calendar and are celebrated in very similar ways.

ROMAN CATHOLICISM

After the Swiss converted to Christianity in the early Middle Ages, Roman Catholics and Protestants waged fierce religious wars in the 16th and 17th centuries. Together, these two groups still account for over 90% of the population, although they now live in harmony.

Roman Catholics form almost half the population of Switzerland. During the Reformation, the rural cantons and the cantons in central Switzerland were not affected by the new ideas of Calvin and Zwingli. Those states now make up the predominantly Catholic areas.

The Roman Catholic and Protestant Churches in Switzerland share a belief in the same God. Their differences are in matters of doctrine and government. The chief differences between the two religions are that Catholics believe in confession and absolution, and revere Mary, the mother of God, in the belief that she will intercede on behalf of the repentant, while Protestants do not accept these doctrines. The government of the Catholic Church is less democratic. Ultimate power lies with the Pope in Rome, and each diocese in a country is governed by a bishop.

Like the Protestant Church, Roman Catholics celebrate the main events of the Christian calendar. Christmas is a public holiday in Switzerland, but for both sects it is a private family affair, with little public activity on the two days of the holiday. Catholic and Protestant children both celebrate St. Nicholas' Day on December 6. Gifts are given, and in some areas, particularly in the Grisons, large and noisy parades take place. On Christmas Eve, Catholic families attend midnight Mass together.

Later in the year, Lent, a period of penitence and fasting, is observed, marking the 40 days that Christ spent in the desert. All public festivals are avoided, and people give up some luxury for the duration. On Easter Sunday, the Resurrection of Christ is celebrated.

In the month of May is Corpus Christi ("KORH-puhs KRIS-tee"), the celebration of the Eucharist, commemorated since 1264. Several towns have parades, with each area stressing different themes in their costumes.

OTHER GROUPS

Besides the Roman Catholic Church, there is another Catholic diocese in Switzerland not associated with it. This is the Old Catholic Church. Differing slightly on matters of doctrine, the group is represented mostly in Bern.

About 20 towns throughout Switzerland have Jewish communities, all linked to the Confederation of Israelite Communities that was established in 1904. They represent about 0.3% of the population.

More recently, Switzerland's need of foreign workers and the huge tide of refugees moving around Europe in the 1980s and 1990s has brought other religions, such as Islam, to Switzerland.

ST. GALLEN

There has been a monastery of some sort at St. Gallen since the traveling Irish monk Gall built a sleeping cell and a wooden church there in the seventh century. During the Middle Ages, the town of St. Gallen became an enormously powerful ecclesiastical center, owning nearby cantons and existing as an independent state. In the 18th century, the monastery and its lands were taken by the French. The monastery became a cathedral in 1847.

The St. Gallen Cathedral (right) represents many different eras of architectural history, with eighth century buildings and a Collegiate Church dating back to the 18th century. The most beautiful room in this complex of buildings is the 18th century abbey library, with its elaborate plasterwork and paintings. It contains some very rare manuscripts, including Irish examples dating back to the period between the seventh and 12th centuries.

Leader of the Reforma-
tion in German-speaking
Switzerland, Huldreich
Zwingli began his work
as preacher, writer, tea-
cher, and social reformer
in Glarus.

HULDREICH ZWINGLI

Born in 1484, Zwingli was a leading figure in the Reformation. He was educated in Basel and then Bern, and intended to enter the Church as a priest. He spent time with the Swiss mercenary armies in Europe and witnessed many deaths. He expressed his opposition to the mercenaries so strongly that he had to retire to the Benedictine abbey at Einsiedeln. Again he found much to criticize in the habits and behavior of the priesthood, and so came to the attention of the City Council of Zurich, which invited him to live and practice his vocation in that city.

His first sermon was electrifying. He outlined a new kind of city-state, where all the elaborate trappings and hypocrisy of the old clergy would be gone. Against the traditions of the priesthood, he married and then set about destroying all the graven images in the churches. He opposed the sale of papal indulgences, a very lucrative activity for the church, and argued with Martin Luther over the nature of the Eucharist, refusing to accept that it might really become the body and blood of Christ. The city of Zurich went along with all his ideas, but its surrounding rural areas rejected them and a war soon followed. In the battle of Kappel, Zurich (1531), he was fatally wounded and his corpse was despoiled, quartered, and burned, and his ashes scattered to the wind.

One of the most important Protestant reformers of the 16th century, John Calvin, also contributed to the Reformation in Switzerland. His ideas profoundly influenced the development of Protestantism in North America and many parts of Europe.

JOHN CALVIN

If Zwingli's work was directed at German Switzerland, then Calvin's was aimed at French Geneva. He was born in Picardy in 1509 and arrived in Geneva some time after 1532, when the town was undergoing a puritan purge. After a brief spell of exile from Geneva, he returned and set about reforming the city. Theologically, Calvin believed in predestination and opposed papal supremacy or any practices not prescribed by the Bible. Politically, he had a much greater impact.

He reorganized life in Geneva, setting up a tribunal of 12 local men to sit in judgment on the morals of their neighbors. People might be called before the tribunal for inappropriate dress or bad conduct, and penalties for frivolous behavior could be severe. Ice-skating, an unusual hairstyle, brightly-colored clothing—all had penalties. Drunkenness, blasphemy, and agnosticism carried the same penalty as murder. Along with the new puritan ideals went a dedication to commerce, and as a result Geneva flourished. Calvin died in 1564, leaving behind a wealthy, but austere city.

LANGUAGE

SWITZERLAND SITS AT THE VERY POINT where three other major cultural regions meet. But its mountainous landscape has meant that whole communities have remained separated and isolated for generations. Consequently, it has four national languages and many regional variations that are so strong that, in some cases, people speaking dialects of the same language cannot understand one another.

Approximately 65% of the population speaks a form of German, 18% speaks French, 10% speaks Italian, and 1% Romansh. Around 6% of the resident population of Switzerland speaks other languages. These people are the foreign workers who come from Spain, Portugal, or elsewhere.

As with the religious makeup of the country, the language groups are not as clearly defined by geography as they once were. Communities of each language group live in all the cities.

Opposite: **Road signs in German, Bern canton. About two-thirds of the total Swiss population speaks German.**

Below: **The language regions of Switzerland.**

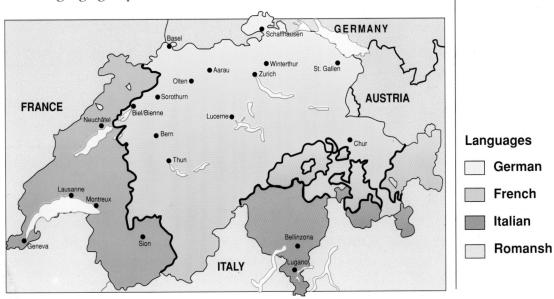

Languages

- German
- French
- Italian
- Romansh

A sign prohibits camping in four languages: German, French, English, and Italian.

NATIONAL AND OFFICIAL LANGUAGES

A country such as Switzerland, with the enormous range of languages spoken within its boundaries, has problems when standard items like official documents, bank notes, or street signs have to be understood by all its citizens. Switzerland has alleviated this problem to a certain extent by having three official languages: German, French, and Italian. All banknotes and official documents are written in all three languages. In addition, Romansh was made a national language in 1938, when Italy was threatening to annex the Romansh-speaking areas. Romansh does not appear on official documents, but it is always the formal form of address in areas where the language is spoken.

The Romansh language evolved in Switzerland when the Rhaeti, an indigenous tribe, came into contact with the conquering Romans. German came to the area with the Alemanni, the tribe that eventually drove out the Romans. Swiss German, based on the language spoken by the Alemanni, evolved along different lines to the standard German spoken in Germany. French came much later when the Burgundians, who occupied southwestern Switzerland, gradually adopted Latin, and this mixture eventually evolved into French.

Later, the situation was complicated by the groups of German-speaking Protestants who settled in the French-speaking Jura. Romansh disappeared from the Rhine valley and was replaced by German, and various patois forms of French developed in the Valais, Jura, and Fribourg areas.

GERMAN AND SWISS GERMAN

In an already complex language situation, German speakers have an even more complicated set of language choices. As we have already seen, the German spoken in Switzerland evolved separately from the German spoken in Germany. Its grammatical structure and much of its vocabulary are different from the language spoken in Germany. In addition, Swiss German has three main dialect groups, as well as many sub-dialects found in isolated valleys and enclaves, so that it is not always possible for the speaker of one German dialect to understand the speaker of another.

The official German used in business and by the civil service is standard German. This is very rarely spoken, although most German speakers understand it, read it in books and daily newspapers, and listen to it on television. News broadcasts are made in standard German, but the sports commentaries are in Swiss German. Swiss German writers tend to write badly in standard German, but have problems with readership if they write in their own dialect. If anything, with its interest in the preservation of old traditions, Switzerland encourages this complexity, and the dialects are heard in more and more official situations.

FRENCH

About 18% of the population of Switzerland speaks French, mostly in the west of Switzerland, in the cantons of Geneva, Vaud, and Neuchâtel. With French the situation is a little less complicated than with the other language groups, since there are fewer surviving dialects. Until recent years there were areas, especially around the Valais and Jura, where a dialect of French similar to Savoyard was spoken. Today, only the older people know this dialect and it is rarely spoken.

ITALIAN AND ITS VARIATIONS

Italian is the official language of Ticino and parts of the Grisons, both relatively small areas of Switzerland. But even within such small communities, there are many different dialects of Italian spoken. Italian dialects are more mutually incomprehensible than German dialects, and there are many different dialects, some more like Lombard (a north Italian dialect) and others closer to Romansh. The situation is complicated by the fact that even within small villages there are also Romansh and German speakers. The official form is standard Italian; this form is used in conversations of an official nature, as well as in documents and on television. Within the same conversation, two speakers may switch between standard Italian and their common dialect as their discussion shifts between official business and more general matters.

ROMANSH

Although Romansh is spoken only by about 50,000 people in the whole of Switzerland, it is one of the country's national languages. As we have seen, it emerged from a combination of the language spoken in the area before the Roman invasion and the Latin of the Roman Empire. The people who lived in the Swiss mountains before the arrival of the Romans are known today as the Rhaetians. Linguistic scholars believe the Romansh language evolved from the Etruscans, a highly sophisticated society from west-central Italy that flourished before the Roman Empire. Romansh is thought, too, to have influences from an even older Celtic language, as well as from Semitic.

There are many dialects of Romansh in Switzerland, the result of the isolation of small communities also typical of other regions of Switzerland.

Of the five different dialects of Romansh, the most widely spoken is the Sursilvan dialect. In the Engadine area of the Grisons, two versions of another dialect known as Ladin are spoken, and in the central Grisons, two dialects, Surmiran and Sutsilvan, are spoken. Romansh is also spoken in the Southern Tyrol in Austria.

Nowadays, all of the Romansh-speaking areas have German-speaking or Italian-speaking majorities. As schools standardize languages and television dominates life, maintaining every single dialect as a living language becomes harder with each generation. The fact that there are so many different versions of Romansh makes the survival of the language even less likely. In addition, there is no major cultural center for the language. Although there was a flowering of Romansh literature in the 19th century, little literature is being produced in modern times. The Swiss government contributes financially to projects aimed at maintaining the language, but like many minority languages around the world, it is seriously threatened by the demands of the more widely-spoken languages.

An Italian restaurant in Mendrisio, in Italian-speaking Ticino.

WHAT'S IN A NAME?

With four national languages, giving things a name that everyone understands can be a difficult activity. Even the major cities are called by different names, depending on what region of Switzerland you are in. The name of the country itself varies according to its languages, being known as Schweiz (German), Suisse (French), and Svizzera (Italian) respectively. The lakes have different names altogether, depending on which language you use.

THE MEDIA

Switzerland publishes the most newspapers per person of any country in the world. There are 275 different newspapers, not including free newspapers or official gazettes. Ticino alone has six different daily newspapers.

In cosmopolitan Zurich, a Swiss bank is given its name in French, Italian, and German.

Six newspapers are read nationally and have a readership of over 100,000. Very few of the newspapers have a particular political ideology, as most are concerned with attracting the largest possible number of readers.

Sixty-nine percent of the population of Switzerland have cable television or its equivalent, and receive around 12 television channels and several radio channels. The Swiss can listen to several international French-speaking and German-speaking channels, and Swiss television offers programs in Italian and Romansh. There are also local television and radio stations.

BIEL

Biel is a town on the shores of Lake Biel, a few miles from the better known Lake Neuchâtel. It is an industrial town, but it also attracts a fair number of tourists. It is a particularly interesting place as far as languages go, because its citizens are more or less evenly distributed between French speakers and German speakers, and it is Switzerland's only officially bilingual town. Many of its citizens are bilingual, speaking both languages well. Here one may hear both languages on and off in the same conversation, as the speakers change topics. Not surprisingly, the town itself has two names, Biel and Bienne, while the lake next to it is called either Lac du Bienne or Bieler See.

ARTS

IN THE MOVIE *THE THIRD MAN*, made just after World War II, Harry Lime, the leading character, cynically defends violence by saying that while the great nations of Europe experienced terrible wars, they also managed to produce great works of art, and that in hundreds of years of peace, all Switzerland managed to produce was the cuckoo clock.

That is a very unfair description of Switzerland, but strangely enough it is the image that many people believe characterizes Switzerland—a safe but dull place that produces only safe but dull things.

Opposite: **A mural decorates the facade of a building in Lucerne.**

Above: **The opera house in Geneva. Although Switzerland is not a leading center of European culture, it has a very active and varied cultural life, as well as many fine museums and theaters.**

In reality, Swiss art forms are dynamic and varied, and Switzerland's safety has convinced many artists to settle there. Switzerland has productive theaters, orchestras, and artists.

Part of Switzerland's image problem is caused by its three major languages. Because Swiss writers use French, German, or Italian, they become part of the school of literature of France, Germany, or Italy rather than of Switzerland itself. It is the same for other fields of artistic endeavor. Many famous Swiss personalities, such as the architect Le Corbusier or the painter and sculptor Alberto Giacometti, are considered French or Italian, despite the fact that they were Swiss-born.

FINE ARTS

Switzerland has produced some of Europe's most famous artists. In the 18th century, Jean-Étienne Liotard and Salomon Gessner produced many worthwhile works of art, while in the 19th century Leopold Robert was famous for his paintings of Italian life. Arnold Böcklin, a painter who worked at the turn of the century, painted symbolic pictures depicting tortured passion. Ferdinand Hodler is considered the father of Swiss landscape painting and did his best work around the turn of the century. He also produced many frescoes depicting events in Swiss history.

In the 20th century, the painter Giovanni Giacometti developed a neo-impressionist style, while his cousin Augusto Giacometti used colors in an innovative way in his landscape paintings. Félix Vallotton created his own distinctive style of painting—a very bold realism. The famous architect Le Corbusier was also Swiss, although little of his architectural designs can be found in Switzerland. He is famous also for his paintings and, with French artist Amédée Ozenfant, created a new school of art called Purism.

Perhaps the most famous Swiss artist of all is Paul Klee, who studied art in Munich and later settled in Germany, forming part of the *Blaue Reiter* (Blue Rider) group. He taught at Bauhaus, a German design school, until 1932, and returned to Switzerland during the rise of Fascism in Germany. Many of his paintings were confiscated by the Nazis. He continued his work in Switzerland, creating small-scale oil paintings such as the abstract "Twittering Machine," which is now in New York City.

Paul Klee's painting "Possibility on the Lake" expresses his philosophy that painting should convey the essential spiritual significance of things and not just familiar reality.

In the period before World War II, some Swiss artists formed a group called the "Allianz" movement, creating abstract concrete art. Sophie Taeuber-Arp, Johannes Itten, Richard Lohse, and Max Bill belonged to this school of art. The very famous dada group of artists also emerged from post-World War I Zurich. The name was chosen at random from a dictionary, and is a French word meaning "rocking horse." The dadaists challenged the established rules of art and used shock tactics to make people think differently about art. There were only a few Swiss artists in the dada group, but they (especially Jean Arp) are still considered an important part of the movement.

A house designed by Le Corbusier. Le Corbusier was one of the main creative forces behind the International school of architecture that influenced 20th-century building trends in the West.

Alberto Giacometti, the son of the Impressionist painter Giovanni Giacometti, has also achieved world fame as a painter and sculptor. He studied in Geneva, but produced most of his work in Paris. In the 1930s he became part of the Surrealist movement, producing abstract symbolic works. His final style consisted of "thin man" statuettes cast in bronze.

Recently, young Swiss artists have begun to explore some dynamic new ideas. Ugo Rondine depicts a sense of the ego in his abstract paintings, while Dieter Wymann takes everyday pieces of furniture and breaks them apart, reassembling them in ways that make one consider the meaning of familiar objects. Albrecht Schneider paints family groups that challenge accepted ideas of formal group paintings. He uses bright colors and arranges his figures in ways that seem to question the security of the family group.

SWISS ARCHITECTURE

One way of tracing the developments in Swiss architectural styles is through religious buildings. The earliest type still existing in Switzerland is the Romanesque style of architecture. Churches in this style were built in the Middle Ages. In Switzerland, the style is characterized by either flat-ceilinged bare rooms supported by pillars or by barrel-vaulted ceilings (round railway tunnel-type ceilings). Later, this simple design was replaced by the Gothic style. The vaulted ceiling became more complex, and highly ornate altars, as well as heavily carved and ornamented furniture, began to make an appearance. There are many Gothic churches throughout the Grisons and in the German-speaking parts of Switzerland.

From the 17th century, a complex, highly ornate new style called Baroque emerged. The Counter-Reformation had begun, and many cantons that had converted to Protestantism were returning to Catholicism and its elaborate church design. Walls were covered in frescoes and paintings. Gilded and carved screens filled the interiors, and paintings of the Virgin

and the saints appeared. The most elaborate Swiss church built in this style is the Collegiate Church of Arlesheim.

In contrast, the modern architectural style is stark and uses reinforced concrete to good effect. An example of this style is the Church of St. Anthony in Basel designed by Karl Moser.

The most famous Swiss architect is Le Corbusier. He did most of his work in Paris and, later, in Germany. Le Corbusier developed a theory of the relationship between modern machine forms and architectural technique. His buildings are typically raised on stilts. He planned areas of the cities of Algiers, Buenos Aires, and Chandigarh, and his influence can be seen in city planning and architecture all over the world.

Opposite and above: **The exterior and interior of the Council House in Basel. Built in the Gothic style, the building was completed in the early 16th century.**

REGIONAL ARCHITECTURE

Every canton in Switzerland has its own distinctive style of house. In the mountains around Bern, houses have low pitched roofs, with wide overhanging eaves, tiled with wooden shingles held in place by stones. The outside of the house is covered in pastoral art, with decorated and carved beams and pillars. This is the typical Swiss chalet of the tourist brochures. In the lowland region of Bern, the houses have an enormous roof reaching down to the second story windows, which creates a large covered area around the house (see picture below).

In the Appenzell region, it rains a great deal and the domestic architecture is designed to deal with this aspect of the weather. The houses and their outbuildings are built in a continuous row so that the inhabitants do not have to walk around in the rain. They have cellars and the roof shingles often cover the walls, too. The gable end of the house always faces the valley.

Around Lucerne the houses are very tall, housing four or five stories, and a steep roof covers the top stories, producing dormer windows (windows projecting from the roof). The front door to the house is on the second story and is approached by means of an outdoor staircase.

In the Valais, the houses are again four or five stories high and built of wood. The kitchen is

usually in a separate building made of stone, attached to the main building by a covered walkway. Long balconies run along the length on one side of the house.

In the Italian-speaking Ticino region, houses are very simple. They are stone-built with very thick walls to support roof tiles made from stone slabs. The staircases to the upper floors are usually on the outside of the house.

PRINTING

Swiss craftsmanship and artistry meet in Swiss printing. Since the Reformation, the Swiss have led the field in this area. In the 16th century Hans Holbein, Niklaus Manuel, and Tobias Stimmer began a tradition of drawing and printmaking by engraving wood that was then dipped in ink and printed. The cut grooves in the wood came out clear on paper while the remaining surface created the design or picture.

This technique continued until the 19th century, when Rudolph Toepffer created the first cartoon strip. By this time the engraving plates were made of copper and given a steel coating. Jean Arp, one of the original dada artists, used the technique, as have Marc Chagall, the Russian painter and designer, and Henry Moore, the English sculptor and graphic artist.

FOLK ART

In a country with so strong a rural tradition as Switzerland, it stands to reason that there should be strong and vibrant folk art. This can be seen in many of Switzerland's folk museums that include the carved and painted farming implements used for the traditional journey to the high pastures in spring. More characteristic are the *Sennenstreifen*, long strips of paper or wood painted in a primitive style and showing the movement of cattle to the high pastures. The pictures often show long lines of cattle, mountains, farm buildings, and herdsmen in traditional costume. These painted strips were hung over the door to the cowshed or even in the living room. In eastern Switzerland the tradition was for *Senntum-Tafelbilder*. These are small paintings of similar motifs usually executed in watercolors on cardboard or paper.

Opposite top and bottom: **Traditional buildings in the Bernese Oberland and the Bernese Mittelland, in the canton of Bern. Every geographical region of Switzerland has its own particular architecture and style of home decor.**

Some of Hesse's more mature writings, such as *Demian,* a novel about troubled adolescence, were influenced by his interest in psychological studies, in particular those of Jung.

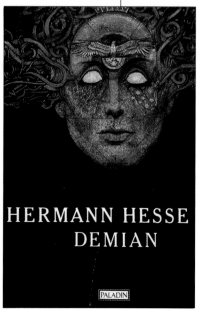

HERMANN HESSE
DEMIAN

PALADIN

SWISS LITERATURE

With three different official languages and a host of dialects as well as Romansh, Switzerland has a varied and interesting literary history. As a neutral and safe state, Switzerland also has been home to many people writing in the Swiss languages who were not native Swiss but whose works were written there.

Switzerland can claim some very famous names in literature. Jean-Jacques Rousseau was born in Geneva and spent most of his life there until the age of 40, when he went to live in Paris and became famous. Hermann Hesse was born in Germany but spent most of his life in Switzerland, where he wrote his major works. While living in Switzerland he was awarded the Nobel Prize for Literature in 1946.

In recent years Max Frisch has become world renowned for his plays that portray Swiss society as restricting and complacent. His major works, written after 1945, have been influenced by the years he spent living in an isolated neutral Switzerland during World War II. Another postwar Swiss, writing in German, is Friedrich Dürrenmatt. His plays also seek to challenge the reassuring qualities of Swiss society that he finds restrictive.

Writing in French in modern times are novelists and poets such as Gustave Roud, Blaise Cendrars, Monique Saint-Hélier, and Catherine Colomb.

Italian Swiss writers have also become famous throughout Europe, notably Felice Filippini, who received the Lugano Prize for Literature in 1943. In Romansh literature, the situation is complex since writers in any of the five main Romance dialects have a tiny audience. However, there are many active writers in the language whose works have been translated.

A portrait of Erasmus by Hans Holbein. Erasmus is credited with the revival of learning and was a proponent of the belief in humanism.

ERASMUS

Erasmus Desiderius was a Dutchman who lived in the 15th century. Although not born Swiss, he lived several years in Switzerland, and many of his important works were written there. He began his life as a monk and later became secretary to the Bishop of Cambrai. He moved from Paris to England but settled eventually in Basel where he wrote his greatest masterpiece, *Colloquia,* which dealt with the wrongs of the Church.

The writings of Erasmus, covering a wide variety of topics, rank him as one of the greatest scholars of his time. The *Adagia*, published in 1508 and containing more than 3,000 proverbs collected from the works of the classical authors, established his reputation. Besides being a noted scholar, Erasmus was also the first editor of the Greek version of the New Testament.

GREAT SWISS THINKERS

Switzerland has produced a large number of people who have made important contributions in the arts and sciences. Three internationally famous Swiss personalities are Jean-Jacques Rousseau ("Jahn-jak ROO-soh"), Carl Gustav Jung ("Karl Goos-TAHV YOONG"), and Jean Piaget ("Jahn Piah-JAY").

JEAN-JACQUES ROUSSEAU (1712–1778) Philosopher, writer, and political theorist, Rousseau was born into a Protestant family in Geneva. He made his outstanding contribution to political philosophy with the publication of *The Social Contract*. This work contains virtually all of Rousseau's political theory. In it he states that the sole basis of every legitimate society is the will of its members; it exists by the consent of the people and is based on a contract among them. The people are sovereign; the government is not their master but their servant, and can always be deposed. Rousseau believed in the natural goodness of people. He loved freedom and hated tyranny. His social and political ideas inspired the leaders of the French Revolution as well as the Romantic generation of the late 18th century. But because the Bern government disapproved of his beliefs, he was forced to leave Switzerland. Rousseau was to live in France for much of his life.

CARL GUSTAV JUNG (1875–1961) A Swiss psychiatrist, Jung was born in 1875 in Kesswil, Switzerland. He studied medicine at Basel University and once he had qualified began to specialize in mental disorders, working first of all at the Burghölzli Mental Institute in Zurich. In 1907, Jung met Sigmund Freud, a neurologist who was also developing some new ideas in Vienna. The two began a close collaboration. In 1911, Freud published his *Psychology of the Unconscious*. This led Jung to reject Freud's ideas about psychoanalysis and develop his own ideas, which he called "analytic psychology."

Jung introduced into psychology the terms "introvert" and "extrovert" that are commonly used to describe shy, withdrawn people and outgoing, sociable people. Another idea of Jung's is that of the collective unconscious or race memory; this is the idea that a person inherits not just the physical characteristics of his or her ancestors but a vestige of ancestral memory. This might explain why very different cultures, divided by time and geography, have similar folk stories or superstitions. Jung is also responsible for the concept of the libido or sexual drive. His work has been influential in psychiatry and in the study of religion, literature, and related fields.

JEAN PIAGET (1896–1980) Born in 1896 at Neuchâtel, Piaget has had an important effect on the school life of most American children as well as children from other parts of the world. At the University of Neuchâtel, he studied zoology and philosophy, receiving his doctorate in 1918. Soon afterward he became interested in psychology and went to Zurich and Paris to study. His ideas on psychology were centered on the way the human infant learns to recognize objects in the world around it and to interact with them. He believed that as each child develops it goes through various stages: the first being physical, as it learns motor skills, the next being intellectual, as it learns language, and the next involving more complex skills such as reading and drawing. Piaget's ideas have influenced educators all over the world.

Piaget worked first as professor of child psychology on the faculty of the University of Geneva in 1929. Later, in 1955, he held the chair in child psychology at the Center for Genetic Epistemology, also in Geneva.

SWISS FILM

The Swiss film industry has come a long way since its early days. A Swiss actor who became famous in European movies is Michel Simon, whose career spanned the years from the early 1930s up to 1971. Michel Simon starred in screen classics such as *Boudu Saved from Drowning* (1932) and *L'Atalante* (1934), a masterpiece directed by the famous French movie director Jean Vigo. Perhaps the most famous Swiss actress is Ursula Andress, who appeared in the James Bond movie *Dr. No,* a cinema classic.

In the last 20 years the small Swiss movie industry has blossomed, producing successful international movies such as Alain Tanner's *Années Lumières* (*The Light Years*), which won the Jury Prize at the Cannes Film Festival in 1981. In German, the critically acclaimed movies have been in the documentary-style, while in French, fiction has dominated. In 1991, Xavier Koller's movie *Reise der Hoffnung* (*Journey of Hope*) won an Oscar. The movie depicted the problems of the enormous number of refugees flooding Europe.

Switzerland now has a thriving film industry supported by state grants that allow well-known movie makers to continue their work and new young directors to prove their talents.

"Man was born free, and everywhere he is in chains."

—*Jean-Jacques Rousseau,*
The Social Contract

LEISURE

IF THERE IS a single national pastime in Switzerland, it is sports. The country has developed an amazing variety of winter and summer sports that attract thousands of tourists each year and fill the leisure hours of Swiss citizens.

Skiing is one of the most widely enjoyed winter activities of Swiss citizens, who seldom have to travel far to enjoy the sport. The mountains also provide bobsledding, mountain walking, and climbing, and in the summer, camping. Shooting is another very popular activity.

In addition to the internationally recognized sports that are popular in Switzerland, there are also some local sports that still make their appearance at the many Swiss festivals. These are Swiss wrestling, farmer's tennis, or *Hornussen* ("horh-NOOS-ehn"), a game similar to baseball but played with disks instead of balls (see p. 103).

Other leisure pursuits include traditional activities such as folk dancing, yodeling, Alpenhorn playing, and attending concerts and the theater. The Swiss certainly need their leisure activities since they are one of the most hardworking peoples in the world, with the Swiss working day one of the longest in Europe.

Opposite: **The Swiss take their cultural heritage seriously and traditional events like Alpenhorn playing are included in their summer leisure activities. Made entirely of pine, the horn is over 10 feet long.**

Above: **A game of chess is played in a park.**

97

Children take skiing lessons at a village ski school.

SKIING

Skiing is a major tourist attraction in Switzerland and the number of places to ski and the varieties of skiing available are countless. The most popular area is probably the Bernese Oberland, where experienced skiers can reach the slopes of the Eiger, Mönch, Jungfrau, and Wetterhorn mountains. Scattered throughout the region are huts with cooking facilities and bunks where skiers can rest overnight as part of a long skiing trip. A mountain railway carries skiers and their equipment into the area and makes the farthest peaks accessible. In winter, after the first snow falls and the danger of avalanches recedes, railway stations are crowded with whole families setting out for a weekend of skiing.

Another region with limitless scope for climbing, ski races, or leisurely travel on skis is the Valais, whose high slopes include the Matterhorn. Snow lies in this area all year round, and it is a very popular place with the Swiss.

Skiing

Skiing can be as expensive or as economical a hobby as each person cares to make it. Places like St. Moritz attract world-famous celebrities, and a stay at some of the resorts there is very expensive. The cost of buying all the latest equipment, as well as the cost of lessons for skiing, can be very high.

A much more popular and less expensive form of skiing is *Langlaufing,* the Swiss name for cross-country skiing. It requires much less skill, and therefore less instruction, and the trails are freely available to whoever wants to use them, eliminating the high resort fees. Every year in March, thousands of skiing enthusiasts gather in the Engadine region of Switzerland for the annual ski marathon, a 26-mile course that stretches from Maloja, past the Engadine lakes, to Zuoz. The race takes about six hours, and in addition to the 11,000 people who take part, many thousands more line the course to watch the competition.

Summer skiing is another popular leisure activity in Switzerland, although, strictly speaking, this is not skiing at all but rather glacier skiing. The ski routes travel along the glaciers that keep their top layer of snow all year round. The activity is confined to the early part of the day, since the glacier surface begins to melt by about lunchtime.

Skiing has given rise to some interesting variations on the basic theme of sliding along on skis. One is ski-joring, being pulled along on skis by Jeep, horse, or even airplane, and another is ski-hang-gliding, where the glider takes off with skis attached to his or her feet and uses the skis to assist in landing.

Constructed in 1898, the Gornergrat Railway leads from Zermatt at 5,332 feet above sea level to the Gornergrat at 10,348 feet. Throughout Switzerland, 550 mountain railways carry skiers to their destinations.

TOBOGGANING

This is a sport that developed in Switzerland at the turn of the century, when bored invalids convalescing in the dry winter air of some of the Swiss mountain resorts took to borrowing local sleds used for pulling packages along in the snow and sliding downhill on them.

In its early stages, the toboggan was a wooden platform with iron strips fixed to the bottom, and the riders sat upright as they slid down the makeshift runs. Later the toboggans began to take on a more aerodynamically sound design, and the riders learned that they could achieve greater speed if they lay flat. By the early 20th century, tobogganers were achieving speeds of 80 miles per hour, and resorts were building complicated toboggan runs in order to attract an influx of people who had heard about the new sport. In 1928, the Winter Olympics were held in St. Moritz, and the toboggan run became one of the events.

Today, the most famous toboggan run is the Cresta Run at St. Moritz. The toboggans are about 50 inches long, 20 inches wide, and four inches thick. Steering is by means of steel hooks that attach to the rider's feet. The runs consist of a series of hairpin bends along a steep ice channel. Experts travel at around 80 miles per hour and complete the distance in just over 55 seconds.

The Cresta Run belongs to the St. Moritz Tobogganing Club. Past and present members of the club include celebrities such as Charlie Chaplin, Errol Flynn, Douglas Fairbanks, and Brigitte Bardot.

CRESTA RUN

Top: **A curling practice session. The game is played on many of Switzerland's frozen lakes.**

Bottom: **A friendly game of ice hockey.**

CURLING

This winter sport is played by two teams of four players who each slide two curling stones on ice toward a target. A stone is rounded on the bottom so it moves easily on ice, has handles of different colors for opposing teams, weighs 40 pounds, is 12 inches across, and 4-5 inches high.

The target, called a house, is a 12-foot circle with a smaller circle at its center. The object is to get the stones as close to the center of the house as possible, and scoring is based on the position of the 16 stones after all the players have had their turn. Each player has two throws alternating with a player from the opposing team. The player's skill lies in the way he or she gets the stone to follow a curved path. Team players improve the stone's direction by using a broom to sweep the ice in front of the stone as it travels. There are complex rules covering penalties and scoring.

Since 1979 the Swiss men's team has been world champion once and the women's team twice.

OTHER WINTER SPORTS

Ice-skating is the second most popular sport in Switzerland. There are about 80 rinks in Switzerland, and around 140 naturally occurring lakes where skating is practiced. Ice hockey is a national pastime, and most towns with a rink have an ice hockey team.

SUMMER ACTIVITIES

Although Switzerland's fame is as a winter sports haven, the Swiss take part in many other sporting activities. For instance, there are over 30 international tennis tournaments throughout the summer, attended by world-famous tennis stars. Much of Switzerland's territory is made up of lakes, and there are many different watersports available for enthusiasts. Hiking and cycling are also frequent activities.

Many traditional pastimes are held during the summer. One of these is Swiss-style wrestling, which takes place in a sand pit and has its own special rules. The two wrestlers wear short linen, leather, or cotton shorts over their everyday pants. The two men grasp each other's torso, with the object of lifting their opponent off the ground, the first man to do so winning the match. Matches often attract as many as 200 contestants and a few thousand spectators.

Swiss farmer's tennis, or *Hornussen,* is played on a large field with eight-foot long wooden bats and a wooden disc instead of a ball. The fielders have to catch the disk with wooden rackets.

Another traditional Swiss game is *Unspunnen Stein* ("oon-SPOON-en stain"), or stone-putting. A player lifts a heavy egg-shaped stone over his head and throws it as far as possible. The sport requires enormous strength.

Watched by a large number of spectators, two contestants compete in a Swiss-style wrestling match.

Rifle shooting and gymnastics are two very popular pastimes. Around one-third of the male population of Switzerland is involved in one of these two activities. Restaurants and cafés often display trophies garnered from local shooting or gymnastics events.

A local game in Switzerland played by children is *Schlagball* ("SHLAG-bawhl"). This game is popular in the canton of Thurgau. It is similar to American softball, except that there are four bases instead of three. There is no pitcher or catcher; the batter throws the ball up and hits it before running around the bases. Another game played by Swiss children is similar to team dodge ball. Two teams face each other across a rectangular field and attempt to eliminate the other team's players by hitting them with the ball.

SOCIAL LIFE

The Swiss are essentially a home-loving people. Evening activities in Switzerland tend to end early, movie theaters begin their last performances around 8 p.m., and the cities are often still and silent by midnight. For many people, relaxing means sitting in a café with a newspaper and a glass of wine or beer, and perhaps a plate of ham or sausage. All the cafés supply newspapers, and newspapers are often found piled on street corners next to a coin box for the honest customers to drop their money in.

In Switzerland there are groups that campaign against alcohol, and many restaurants do not serve it. Gambling, too, is frowned upon. There are casinos, but there are no places like Las Vegas. The commonest form of gambling is *boule* ("BOOL"), a kind of roulette. The maximum stake allowed is five francs, which makes it very difficult for anyone to win a fortune—or lose one either.

Much Swiss social life revolves around the family. Friends and family often get together at one another's homes rather than go out to eat. Concerts are very popular, and many Swiss people take an active part in summer performances that feature folk singing. There are many choral societies, and yodeling clubs exist where men practice the Alpine art of yodeling, raising the voice suddenly from one pitch to another. Whereas in other countries traditional costumes, dances, and singing exist especially for the tourists, the Swiss have genuine interest in these aspects of their heritage and their festivals are not tourist-oriented.

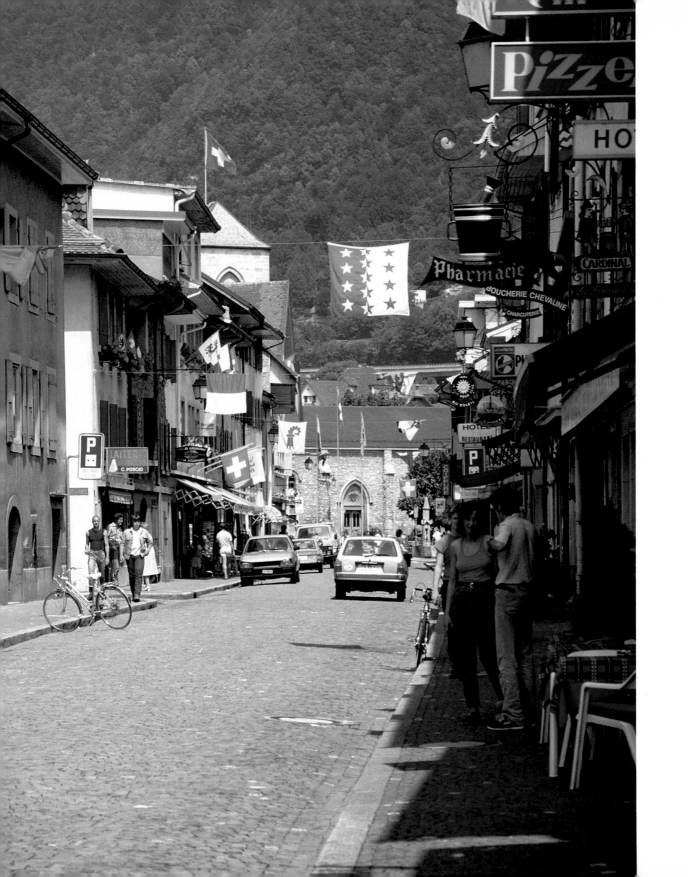

FESTIVALS

SWITZERLAND HAS MANY FESTIVALS that are related to events in the Christian calendar, the passage of the seasons, or events in Switzerland's history. They are colorful and yet sedate; the Swiss like to observe ancient customs but deplore waste or excess. In 1991, Switzerland celebrated its 700th anniversary as a confederation, but four years previously, the people in several of the central cantons voted against any spectacular displays since these would be environmentally harmful and extravagant. In the end, the year-long celebrations were marked by small festivals in each village, with displays of traditional Swiss skills such as yodeling and flugelhorn playing, exhibitions, and concerts rather than any huge centralized displays or celebrations.

There are over 100 different festivals celebrated in Switzerland. Many originated in a pagan time before the arrival of Christianity, and this can be seen in their rituals, which include driving away evil spirits, seeking blessings for the harvest, or driving away the last of winter.

Opposite: **The streets of Switzerland are decorated with flags on the Swiss National Day, August 1.**

Below: **In Küssnacht village, participants in enormous bishop's miters (official headdresses) take part in a procession to celebrate St. Nicholas' Day.**

Dressed in black and red costumes, three Santa Clauses entertain to raise money for charity.

RELIGIOUS FESTIVALS

In common with other European countries, Switzerland's religious calendar begins on December 6, when the feast of St. Nicholas is celebrated. The tradition of giving gifts, which has largely moved over to Christmas Eve, began with this saint's day. St. Nicholas is the patron saint of youth, and gifts were given in honor of his traditional generosity.

In Küssnacht and Arth, processions are held with participants wearing huge hats or bishop's miters illuminated from the inside. Festivities carry on through the night, with people celebrating in bars and wandering the streets cracking whips, blowing horns, and ringing bells. Christmas time in Switzerland has much of the glitter and celebration of an American Christmas.

The next event in the Christian calendar is Lent, and around that time Switzerland abounds with festivals, the origins of most of which are completely lost. In villages around Lötschental, the *Roitschäggätä* are people dressed up in hideous masks and goatskins, carrying cowbells. They run around the villages making a lot of noise to scare away all the evil spirits. Other areas also celebrate their own versions of this event.

In Basel and Zurich, three days before Ash Wednesday (the beginning of Lent), tens of thousands of masked people take part in the *Fastnacht* festival, an event which has similarity to the Mardi Gras festival in New Orleans, Louisiana. *Fastnacht* marks the last days before Lenten abstinence and is celebrated with great revelry. The dramatic and colorful festival begins at 4 a.m. when all the lights in the city are put out and groups of people carrying oil lanterns travel the streets beating drums and playing pipes. The participants wear masks, and their elaborate costumes

add to the carnival spirit. The festival continues for three days with decorated floats and more pipe-and-drum bands.

On Maundy Thursday, the eve of Good Friday, Christ's washing of His disciples' feet is celebrated in Catholic communities, and in Fribourg the bishop, as a token of humility, kisses the feet of the faithful in the cathedral.

On Good Friday there are many religious processions in the towns of southern Switzerland. In Mendrisio, a passion play is enacted on Maundy Thursday and Good Friday. On Ascension Day in Lucerne, in a ceremony dating back to 1509, priests carrying the holy sacrament ride around the village on horseback, blessing the crops.

The next event in the religious calendar is Corpus Christi in May. In Appenzell, the streets are strewn with carpets of flowers, and in Kippel in the Valais, the Grenadiers of God, in 19th-century uniforms, march through the town to commemorate the event. In Romont in western Switzerland, part of the procession is a group of shrouded weeping women carrying representations of Christ's shroud, crown of thorns, and other things associated with the crucifixion.

Participants, dressed in colorful costumes and masks, march through the streets of Basel during the *Fastnacht festival*. It is a time for merrymaking before the observance of Lent, when indulgences (such as meat eating and excessive revelry) must be given up.

In January, following an old custom in the Engadine, children are carried on sleds decorated with wreaths of evergreens and homemade paper roses.

FOLK FESTIVALS

In Switzerland, it is sometimes difficult to distinguish religious festivals from folk festivals since the two calendars of events have, over the centuries, become connected with one another. Many of the rites have their origin in rituals much older than Christianity.

The folk festival year begins in January, when in Urnäsch, *Silvesterklause* ("Spirits of the New Year") go from house to house to wish families a prosperous year. Participants in traditional costume wear cowbells, masks, and glowing headgear that are often huge and illustrate scenes from rural life. In the middle of January in the Engadine, unmarried boys and girls in traditional costume travel in decorated sleds from one village to another. In Basel, the *Vogel Gryff* (Griffin) festival celebrates community ties, depicted by three symbolic figures: the wild man of the woods, a lion, and a griffin (a mythical lion with eagle's head). Accompanied by mummers, or merrymakers dressed in masks and strange costumes, the three characters mark the occasion by dancing and parading in the streets.

February sees more mummers in Basel at the *Fastnacht* parade, and in Schwyz, where they dress as harlequins called *Blatzi*. In several villages, festivals take place in which Old Man Winter, in one form or another, is paraded through town and burned. In Zurich, the figure is a straw scarecrow called *Boogg*. This symbol of wintertime, of which everyone is weary, is then burned by the side of Lake Zurich.

May Day is an important folk event all over Europe, and in Switzerland many small villages hold festivals. In Geneva two children, a boy and a girl, are named the May King and Queen. They are solemnly crowned on the second Sunday of May, and lead a procession from house to house through their home village.

June sees the return of the cows to the high pastures in regions such as the Valais, Gruyère, and Appenzell, and the event is surrounded by many festivities and rituals. The men who herd the animals dress in traditional costume and decorate their cows with flowers and bells. There are flag-tossing competitions, Alpenhorn playing, traditional dances, and Swiss wrestling. In the lower Valais, there are cow fights in which cows are rarely harmed, but the winning cow becomes queen of the herd and wears an enormous cowbell.

Fall brings harvest festivals throughout the rural regions of Switzerland. These are accompanied by flower processions, especially in Geneva, Lugano, and Neuchâtel.

Cattle herders take their cows up to the summer pastures to feed. Both the trip up and the return to the valley give rise to much celebration.

FESTIVALS FROM HISTORY

Several of the festivals celebrated by the Swiss have their origin in some historical event. Swiss National Day, August 1, celebrates the meeting in the field at Rütli, where the first Swiss cantons forged a defensive alliance in 1291. The day is celebrated with readings of the federal pact, torchlight processions, fireworks, and bonfires throughout the country.

In July, the story of William Tell is retold in Johann Schiller's 18th century play, *Wilhelm Tell*, in Interlaken. In December, Geneva celebrates the *Escalade*, which remembers the day in 1602 when the Duke of Savoy tried to conquer the city using ladders to climb the city walls. Every year, the town of Sempach celebrates the Battle of Sempach in 1386, when a small Swiss force was able to defeat Duke Leopold III of Austria. National costume is worn and the armor of the time is dusted off for the festivities.

A poster announces the date of a festival in Geneva.

MODERN FESTIVALS

Switzerland has many festivals whose origins are recent. In 1938, Toscanini began a music festival at Lucerne, and each year world-famous orchestras and conductors come to the city to perform in the concert hall by the lake. Zurich has a music festival where the emphasis is on opera, and Montreux and Gstaad also have classical music festivals.

Zurich also holds a jazz festival and an arts festival in June, with all the arts represented. There are concerts, art exhibitions, operas, and plays in all the national languages, as well as folk music and street theater and musicians. Montreux holds a very prestigious television festival, where all the European countries submit entries for the Golden Rose of Montreux Award.

FÊTES DE GENÈVE

du 12 au 15 Août

FOOD FESTIVALS

Harvest is an occasion for festivals that celebrate the year's crops. In the wine-growing areas, there are many wine festivals such as the one at Vevey, which is celebrated only rarely, four times in this century. The festival dates back to the Middle Ages when there was a winemaker's guild. This guild awarded prizes to the best workers in the vineyards, who were paraded through the town. By the 17th century, the event had become a celebration of the wine god, Bacchus, with the god himself portrayed in the procession by a small boy seated on a barrel. Ceres, a goddess, was also represented, as were Noah and several figures from mythology. More recent festivals have added fife and drum bands from Basel and herdsmen from Gruyère. The last festival was in 1977 and was a very elaborate affair. The procession was followed by a gigantic party that is still talked about with pleasure today!

In the Bernese Oberland, a new festival has been created by an old tradition. It was, and still is, common for the farmers of the region to pool their milk in order to make cheese. Once the cheese is ready at the end of summer, it is given out to each farmer in accordance with the milk produced by his cows. Once upon a time it may have been a simple operation, but today it has been turned into an event, with stalls selling the cheese and lots of wine and food served to the accompaniment of music.

The annual distribution of cheese is an occasion for celebration in the Bernese Oberland.

FOOD

SWISS COOKING IS AS VARIED as the races of the people that make up the country. It is an interesting mix of French, German, and Italian cooking with some indigenous dishes thrown in. The Swiss kitchen contains fewer convenience foods than its U.S. equivalent, and the Swiss shop carefully for fresh vegetables in the green markets that still fill the towns and cities.

Staples vary from area to area, but the potato is ubiquitous. In the Italian-speaking Ticino area, rice is the staple, while polenta, a dish made from corn, is also popular. Switzerland is of course famous for its cheeses. It produces its own wine and many forms of dried and cured meat. The best known aspect of Swiss cuisine is fondue ("fahn-doo"), a dish of melted cheese and wine served with bread.

Opposite and above: **Fruits and vegetables in the green markets of Switzerland's towns and cities. While livestock farming is confined mostly to the mountain regions, farm produce such as shown here is grown in the central plateau and the lower Alpine valleys.**

REGIONAL DISHES

Regionally, the cuisines of Switzerland follow the linguistic makeup of the country. In the west of Switzerland, cooking styles have French influence, in the south, Italian dishes predominate, while the rest of the country tends to have German-oriented cuisine.

In the west, fish dishes are the speciality. Bernese salmon or many of the freshwater fish such as char, grayling, and trout are simply cooked in butter. Mushrooms are also important in western Swiss cooking and mushroom sauce is used for a variety of dishes. The west specializes in cured pork, too, from various sausages to smoked ham and pork chops. Pig's feet cooked in Madeira wine are a speciality of Geneva.

A Swiss family having a meal of fondue. Most Swiss own a fondue set— a deep ceramic dish on a rack over a burner.

In Lucerne, Zug, and other parts of central Switzerland, a popular regional dish is cheese soup. A Zurich speciality is a meat stew made from strips of meat cooked for a long time and served with the German form of *rösti* (pan-roasted potatoes). *Ratsherentopf* ("rahts-HAIR-un-topf") is another Zurich dish made from several different stewed meats and potatoes.

In the Valais or the Grisons, dried meats are expensive and much in demand. The meat is hung in the arid air of the mountain slopes and left to dry out completely. It is not smoked. The meat is sliced very thinly and served with pickled onions or gherkins as an hors d'oeuvre.

In Bern and the Rhine cantons, veal is popular and often cooked in cream sauce and served with noodles. Another speciality of this area is *Mistkratzerli,* a dish of young rooster served with baked potatoes. St. Gallen and Basel are famous for their own variety of sausage.

Ticino is famous for its rice and noodles, as one would expect of an Italian-speaking region. *Busecca*, a soup made from tripe, and a dish of snails served with walnuts are also Ticino specialities.

CAKES AND PASTRIES

All over Switzerland, the pastry shops are filled with cakes and pastries from the many regions of the country. The most widely sold cakes are called *leckerli*, which are flat and oblong spiced honey cakes topped with a coating of sugar icing. They vary from place to place, being made with bear-shaped candies on the top in Bern. *Gugelhopf* is another regional cake that is popular all over Switzerland. It is a large bun with a hollow center that is often filled with whipped cream. *Birnbrot* is a teabread made with dried fruits, while *fladen* and *krapfen* ("KRAHP-fen") are richer fruit cakes filled with nuts, almond paste, and pears. *Kirschtorte* ("KIRSH-torta") from Zug has become another national favorite. As its name suggests, it is a cherry tart. From the Engadine comes *nusstorte,* a layer cake made with nut dough.

A bakery in a French-speaking area offers all kinds of desserts including cakes and cookies.

THE POTATO

It is not only the Irish who have made great use of the potato. Arriving in Switzerland sometime in the 17th century, the potato soon became a very important part of the Swiss diet. Unlike the Irish, the Swiss did not stop at boiling them whole and serving them with butter. In Swiss cooking, potatoes are rarely served in this way or even as French fries. They are cooked whole in their skins or boiled, and then pureed, piped on to baking trays, and baked to make potatoes au gratin, or they are boiled, diced, dried, and then roasted to make *rösti*. Potatoes are also an important element of the cheese dish raclette ("rah-KLEHT").

Above: **A cheese cellar.**

Below: **Emmentaler, better known as Swiss cheese, is made in the German part of Switzerland.**

SWISS CHEESE

Swiss cheese is famous because of Emmentaler, the cheese with the large round holes running through it. But there are many other types of Swiss cheeses than this one type.

Emmentaler has its enormous holes because of the way it is made. Over the four months that the cheese is left to ferment, it produces carbonic acid that forms into bubbles, and as the cheese sets, the bubbles become fixed within it. To tell if the cheese has developed properly, you must look at the shape of the holes. If they are regular in shape and perfectly round, then the cheese has fermented well and will taste good. Roman writers who traveled through this area described the holes in the cheese. This is proof that Emmentaler is a very old type of cheese.

Gruyère is another very famous Swiss cheese. Others are not so well known. Tête de Moine is a soft cheese made in a cone-shaped block from which the cheese is scraped. Vacherin, a cream cheese made in the Jura, is stored in round boxes made from birchbark. It ripens during the summer and is ready by November.

Raclette is a dish made from melted Swiss cheeses, mostly *bagnes* and *conches* cheeses made in the Valais. The cheeses are cut in half and left by an open fire to melt. When they are ready, they are poured over potatoes boiled in their skins and served with pickled spring onions and gherkins. Other cheese dishes are *salés au fromage*, cheese quiche, and cheesecake.

FONDUE

The cantons of Valais, Vaud, and Geneva all claim to have originated this famous Swiss dish. It first came to the United States in 1939, when it was brought to the Swiss pavilion of the New York World's Fair. The basic ingredients of the dish are Gruyère and Emmentaler cheese, garlic, flour, white wine, and kirsch (a cherry liqueur). The cooking pot is rubbed with the garlic clove and the cheese is slowly melted over a stove with the wine and kirsch. When the cheese is fully melted, the pot is brought to the table and kept at a bubbling temperature over a flame. Diners each have a plate of chunks of white bread that they spear on a long, two-pronged fork and dunk into the sauce. As the sauce boils away, it gets stronger and better. Traditionally, the person who lets bread fall into the pot has to buy a bottle of white wine for all the diners.

CHEESE FONDUE NEUCHÂTELOISE

8 ounces Emmentaler cheese
8 ounces Gruyère cheese
5 tablespoons flour
1 large clove garlic
$1/2$–$3/4$ pint dry white wine
2–4 tablespoons kirsch
freshly ground black pepper
cubes of French bread

Grate the cheeses and mix with the flour. Rub the fondue pot or saucepan with the clove of garlic. Leave the garlic in the pot, heat the pot, and add the wine. Bring to a boil. Lower the heat and begin adding the cheese and flour mixture, stirring all the time with a wooden spoon. As the cheese melts, a thick sauce will develop. Add the kirsch, season with pepper, and serve, keeping the pot hot over a burner, but without letting it boil. Spear the bread cubes on long forks and dip into the sauce.

SWISS WINES

Not as famous as French or German wines, Swiss wines rarely travel abroad because they are in such great demand in Switzerland itself that the supply does not cover the demand. People in the west and south of the country consume more wine than the German-speaking areas, where they consume more beer. It is thought that the grapevine was first brought to Switzerland by the Romans. The Swiss make mostly white wine in the Valais, Vaud, and Neuchâtel regions, where the long dry summers favor vine growing. Ticino grows mostly black grapes that make the red wines. Until the 1950s Swiss wine was of poor quality. But a statute was passed at that time, imposing strict quality controls over wine growers, and from then on the wines have vastly improved.

A CULINARY CALENDAR

Many traditional Swiss dishes are linked to the cultural events of the year. At New Year, the traditional dish in Ticino is *zampone*, stuffed pig's feet cooked with lentils. In the Grisons, smoked pork with vegetables in barley soup is eaten at that time.

Shrove Tuesday brings deep fried crisp wafers of pastry. In the Ticino, whole villages bring out huge pots in which they cook risotto, stirring it constantly with enormous wooden spoons. It is served with garlic-flavored pork sausages. At Easter, the traditional dish is lamb or kid, and it is customary for families to go off to the countryside to pick dandelion greens for their salads.

In fall, when the shooting season starts, chamois is on the menu. Before the use of feed grain made it possible to keep animals alive over the winter, huge amounts of meat become available in the markets in the fall, and smoked and cured meats still abound during this period. One dish common at this time is *Bernerplatte,* which consists of cured and smoked meats served with potatoes and sauerkraut or French green beans.

Risotto, which is rice cooked in broth and flavored with grated cheese, is also served with mushrooms.

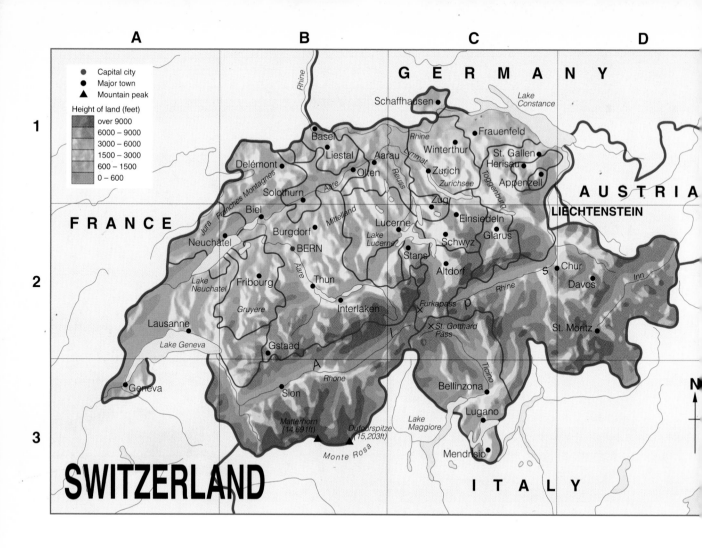

Legend:

- ● Capital city
- ● Major town
- ▲ Mountain peak

Height of land (feet)

- over 9000
- 6000 – 9000
- 3000 – 6000
- 1500 – 3000
- 600 – 1500
- 0 – 600

G E R M A N Y

Schaffhausen

Lake Constance

Rhine

Frauenfeld

Basel

Rhine

Winterthur

St. Gallen

Liestal

Limmat

Herisau

Delémont

Aarau

Zurich

Appenzell

Olten

Zurichsee

A U S T R I A

Solothurn

Reuss

Zug

LIECHTENSTEIN

Aare

Mittelland

Biel

Einsiedeln

Lucerne

Burgdorf

Lake Lucerne

Glarus

Neuchâtel

Schwyz

BERN

Stans

S

Chur

Lake Neuchâtel

Altdorf

Rhine

Davos

Fribourg

Aare

Thun

Inn

Furkapass

ρ

Interlaken

Gruyere

St. Gotthard Pass

Lausanne

Ι

St. Moritz

Lake Geneva

Gstaad

Α

Bellinzona

Ticino

Geneva

Sion

Rhone

Lugano

Lake Maggiore

Matterhorn (14,691ft)

Dufourspitze (15,203ft)

Mendrisio

Monte Rosa

I T A L Y

F R A N C E

Jura

Franches Montagnes

N

SWITZERLAND

A   B   C   D

1

2

3

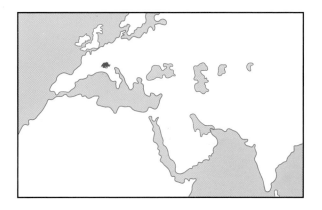

QUICK NOTES

LAND AREA
15,943 square miles, including 523 square miles of inland water

POPULATION
6,674,000, approximately 418 people to the square mile

CAPITAL
Bern

NATIONAL ANTHEM
The Swiss Psalm

FLAG
White cross on red background

FORM OF GOVERNMENT
Federal republic

POLITICAL DIVISIONS
Zurich, Bern, Lucerne, Uri, Schwyz, Obwalden, Nidwalden, Glarus, Zug, Fribourg, Solothurn, Basel-Town, Basel-Country, Schaffhausen, Appenzell Outer-Rhodes, Appenzell Inner-Rhodes, St. Gallen, Grisons, Aargovia, Thurgovia, Ticino, Vaud, Valais, Neuchâtel, Geneva, Jura

MAJOR CITIES
Zurich, Basel, Geneva, Lausanne

HIGHEST POINT
Dufourspitze, at 15,203 feet

LOWEST POINT
Shores of Lake Maggiore, 633 feet above sea level

MAJOR RIVERS
Aare, Rhine, Rhone, Inn, Ticino

OFFICIAL LANGUAGES
German, French, Italian. Romansh is a national language.

MAJOR RELIGIONS
Roman Catholicism, Protestantism

CURRENCY
Swiss franc
(US$1 = 1.81 Swiss francs)

MAIN EXPORTS
Machinery, watches, pharmaceuticals, chemicals

NATIONAL DAY
August 1

GLOSSARY

Alpenhorn Long, powerful horn of wood or bark used chiefly by Swiss herdsmen for communicating in the Alps.

Corpus Christi ("KORH-puhs KRIS-tee") Roman Catholic festival in honor of the Eucharist or Holy Communion.

Fastnacht ("FAHS-nahkt") A festival celebrated before the beginning of Lent.

fondue ("fahn-doo") A popular Swiss dish of melted cheese, usually flavored with white wine and kirsch, a cherry liqueur.

Hornussen ("horh-NOOS-ehn") Often called "farmer's tennis," this traditional Swiss sport has a vague similarity to American baseball.

Landsgemeinde ("LAHNTS-ger-min-de") The outdoor parliament held in spring when citizens vote for their representatives.

polenta ("poh-LEHN-tah") A kind of gruel made from cornmeal.

predestination The belief that human beings have no control over events because they have already been decided by God or by fate.

raclette ("rah-KLEHT") Melted cheese served with potatoes.

Romansh ("roh-MANSH") Language spoken primarily in eastern Switzerland.

rösti ("ROHRS-tee") Pan-roasted potatoes.

Schlagball ("SHLAG-borhl") Game similar to American softball.

Sonderbund Separatist league formed on December 11, 1845, by seven Catholic Swiss cantons to oppose anti-Catholic measures by Protestant liberal cantons. The term Sonderbund also refers to the civil war that resulted from this conflict.

Schwyzerdütsch ("SHVEET-zur-dootch") A term given to Swiss German dialect languages.

Unspunnen Stein ("oon-SPOON-en stain") Swiss shot-putting.

BIBLIOGRAPHY

Hadley, L.: *Fielding's Europe with Children,* William Morrow, New York, 1984.

Hintz, Martin: *Switzerland—Enchantment of the World,* Children Press, Chicago, 1986.

Lye, Keith (ed): *Today's World—Europe,* Gloucester Press, New York, 1984.

Schrepfer, Margaret: *The Summit of Europe,* Dillon Press, Minneapolis, 1989.

INDEX

INDEX

INDEX

PICTURE CREDITS